Editor-in-Chief and Founder:
    Lyndon H. LaRouche, Jr.
Editorial Board: *Lyndon H. LaRouche, Jr. , Helga
    Zepp-LaRouche, Robert Ingraham, Tony
    Papert, Gerald Rose, Dennis Small, Jeffrey
    Steinberg, William Wertz*
Co-Editors: *Robert Ingraham, Tony Papert*
Managing Editor: *Nancy Spannaus*
Technology: *Marsha Freeman*
Books: *Katherine Notley*
Ebooks: *Richard Burden*
Graphics: *Alan Yue*
Photos: *Stuart Lewis*
Circulation Manager: *Stanley Ezrol*

INTELLIGENCE DIRECTORS
Counterintelligence: *Jeffrey Steinberg, Michele
    Steinberg*
Economics: *John Hoefle, Marcia Merry Baker,
    Paul Gallagher*
History: *Anton Chaitkin*
Ibero-America: *Dennis Small*
Russia and Eastern Europe: *Rachel Douglas*
United States: *Debra Freeman*

INTERNATIONAL BUREAUS
Bogotá: *Miriam Redondo*
Berlin: *Rainer Apel*
Copenhagen: *Tom Gillesberg*
Houston: *Harley Schlanger*
Lima: *Sara Madueño*
Melbourne: *Robert Barwick*
Mexico City: *Gerardo Castilleja Chávez*
New Delhi: *Ramtanu Maitra*
Paris: *Christine Bierre*
Stockholm: *Ulf Sandmark*
United Nations, N.Y.C.: *Leni Rubinstein*
Washington, D.C.: *William Jones*
Wiesbaden: *Göran Haglund*

ON THE WEB
e-mail: eirns@larouchepub.com
www.larouchepub.com
www.executiveintelligencereview.com
www.larouchepub.com/eiw
Webmaster: *John Sigerson*
Assistant Webmaster: *George Hollis*
Editor, Arabic-language edition: *Hussein Askary*

EIR (ISSN 0273-6314) *is published weekly
(50 issues), by EIR News Service, Inc.,
P.O. Box 17390, Washington, D.C. 20041-0390.
(703) 777-9451*

European Headquarters: E.I.R. GmbH, Postfach
Bahnstrasse 9a, D-65205, Wiesbaden, Germany
Tel: 49-611-73650
Homepage: http://www.eirna.com
e-mail: eirna@eirna.com
Director: Georg Neudecker

Montreal, Canada: 514-461-1557

Denmark: EIR - Danmark, Sankt Knuds Vej 11,
basement left, DK-1903 Frederiksberg, Denmark.
Tel.: +45 35 43 60 40, Fax: +45 35 43 87 57. e-mail:
eirdk@hotmail.com.

Mexico City: EIR, Sor Juana Inés de la Cruz 242-2
Col. Agricultura C.P. 11360
Delegación M. Hidalgo, México D.F.
Tel. (5525) 5318-2301
eirmexico@gmail.com

Canada Post Publication Sales Agreement
#40683579

Postmaster: Send all address changes to *EIR*, P.O.
Box 17390, Washington, D.C. 20041-0390.

Signed articles in *EIR* represent the views of the
authors, and not necessarily those of the Editorial
Board.

Obama's Plan
For Mass Murder
In January

January First Is Doomsday! Only an FDR Action Can Save You from Disaster

Dec. 23—President Barack Obama and the entire U.S. Congress have betrayed you, the American people, by refusing, out of cowardice, to take the necessary emergency actions to prevent the greatest financial and economic crash—far worse than 1929 and 2008—from happening in the hours and days just ahead. Unless you, the American people, stand up and demand immediate action, the nation, and much of mankind, is facing catastrophe as the New Year begins.

The entire trans-Atlantic financial system is about to blow. In the past few weeks, $15 billion in junk and investment grade bonds have been wiped out. This is but a harbinger of an imminent total crash of the trans-Atlantic financial bubble. As of Jan. 1, a $72 billion debt bubble is set to explode in Puerto Rico. Congress had the opportunity to act to prevent this before leaving town, but failed to do so.

An estimated $5 trillion in debt, tied to the collapsing U.S. domestic shale oil and gas sector, is blowing up. In Western Canada, this bubble has already been shattered, triggering mass unemployment—100,000 jobs gone in 2015, the equivalent of 750,000 jobs lost in the United States—a crash of the real estate market, and a social breakdown. That same crisis is coming to the United States, at an accelerating rate, but on a much larger scale.

In Europe, starting on Jan. 1, 2016, new laws go into effect, eliminating all protections for bank depositors, who will have their savings stolen under "bail-in" regulations, as has already happened in Cyprus. More than 10,000 Italian depositors had their savings "bailed in" (expropriated) in the collapse of four banks this month. The same measures are included in the Dodd-Frank bill here in the United States. If your bank collapses, your life savings can be stolen to save the bank. It can and will happen here, thanks to the cowardice and corruption of your elected officials, who have kept you in the dark and violated their oaths of office.

Congress had the chance, before leaving town, to prevent this now on-rushing crisis. They were warned. They could have passed bills, already introduced in both Houses of Congress to reinstate Glass-Steagall, the FDR legislation that broke up the Depression era too-big-to-fail banks, by separating commercial banking from gambling activities. But Congress was bought out by Wall Street and failed you.

President Obama is a wholly-owned creature of Wall Street and London. Wall Street is hopelessly bankrupt, and they intend to cling to power by stealing your money, wiping out your health care, and shutting down what is left of the real economy. Within days or weeks, you could be facing food shortages, hyperinflation, and a complete breakdown of everything you think of as normal.

President Obama, on behalf of Wall Street and London, is also provoking confrontation with Russia, driving the world towards global war, a war that some top American and Russian military commanders warn could rapidly become a war of thermonuclear extinction.

On Jan. 1, 2016, under U.S. and International Monetary Fund approval, Ukraine will default on $3 billion in debt to Russia, an act of open Western provocation against Moscow, on top of the already ongoing sanctions, the eastward expansion of NATO, and other acts of direct military provocation.

This is deadly serious. The world is on the cusp of a worse than Great Depression crash and a new world war. You must now act because your elected officials have abandoned you out of cowardice and corruption. They, along with President Obama, deserve your derision and anger, for their cowardly behavior.

There are solutions readily available. Wall Street must be shut down immediately. Not one penny more to bail out these criminals! Congress must remove Wall Street puppet Barack Obama from office, through impeachment, or through invoking the 25th Amendment, which provides for the removal of a President from office who is mentally unfit to continue to serve. Glass-Steagall must be immediately reinstated, and a series of initiatives must be taken, all modeled on what the great American President Franklin Roosevelt did in his first months in office, to create millions of productive jobs, rebuild the nation's collapsed infrastructure, and restore our dignity.

Congress can take these actions in a matter of hours, but they will only act in time if you wake up and demand it.

The alternative is Hell on Earth by the start of the New Year. Do you, your friends, your neighbors, have the moral fitness to survive? That is the question on your table this Christmas Eve.

Evil Rulers Are Bringing Us to Annihilation; January 1 Will Be the Trigger

Dec. 25—The mega-financial blow-out, which is now scheduled immediately after New Year's Day, promises an almost-instant shutdown of the economies of the United States, Western Europe, and most of Central and South America. It will be immeasurably worse than that of 2008 or 1929.

The most recent case which compares with the disaster we face over the coming few days, is Europe's catastrophe of the Fourteenth Century. Then as now, a long-term rotting-out of culture prepared the way for a series of savage, anti-human acts by actually Satanic rulers which suddenly precipitated the collapse of society and mass death. Amidst perpetual warfare, a series of famines early in the century helped to prepare the way for the evil which followed. In 1344, the Lombard banking houses of the Bardi and Peruzzi declared bankruptcy, whereupon the Venetian banking network closed down the entire economic system of Europe, forcing conditions which further decimated the populations' resistance to disease. The Black Death (bubonic plague) struck in 1347. Its successive waves are estimated to have killed off 60% of Europe's population.

And now, today, in the aftermath of the vast cultural downslide called the Twentieth Century, three Satanic rulers are leading us to our immediate destruction: Queen Elizabeth, Barack Obama, and Pope Francis.

The Queen-Empress Elizabeth II is a far more knowingly evil figure than her ancestor George III, who murdered our patriots over 200 years ago. She represents the British Empire of the Twentieth Century, of the Lord Bertrand Russell who legislated an end to science and art in favor of dead mathematics. Like Russell, she and her husband advocate worldwide savage population-reduction, by whatever means. That was the not-so-secret agenda of her just-concluded Paris conference on supposed man-made climate change.

The Satanism of Queen Elizabeth and her like is their drive to extinguish the "divine spark" in man,—that which makes man in "the living image of God." In other words, humanity.

It should make every Catholic ashamed,—indeed, every Christian,—that Pope Francis adopted the anti-human credo of the British Empire in his insane, raving so-called Encyclical "Laudato Si'." He has fought for it ever since. Whatever his reasons, he has disqualified himself as Pope, even as a simple priest.

Our so-called President Barack Obama is a puppet of this Queen-Empress, controlled by the British Monarchy through Valerie Jarrett, who was the one who tapped him to be President in the first place, when he was an obscure State Senator. It was British monarchy-controlled drug money which gave Obama a crooked victory over popular favorite Hillary Clinton in the 2008 Democratic Primaries. (Unfortunately, Hillary has destroyed all her own qualifications since becoming Obama's puppet after his election.)

Obama was trained to be a mass-murderer by his Indonesian step-father Lolo Soetoro. Now, every Tuesday, he presides over a White House meeting to decide on a new list of people to murder,—including American citizens. The reason that the major press—such as the *New York Times* and the *Wall Street Journal*—gives him a free pass is that they're afraid he'll murder them too. He probably will.

Congressmen share the same, justified, fear,—but they have no excuse. The oath they took to the Constitution is a soldier's oath. If they will not immediately remove Obama and shut down Wall Street, they are not real Congressmen at all.

In short, your leaders have sold you out to the Devil. Your Congressmen have sold you out, in the best cases, out of fear. But the solutions which Franklin Roosevelt applied in 1932-33, in a far milder crisis, are still available today. Only a child would talk about the "odds"; obviously the odds are against us. So what?

EIR Contents

www.larouchepub.com Volume 43, Number 1, January 1, 2016

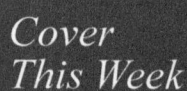

Cover This Week

From Pieter Bruegel the Elder's Triumph of Death, painted in 1562

EU Policy Is Deadly: For Your Bank Account and the Refugees

by Helga Zepp-LaRouche, chair of the German political party Civil Rights Movement Solidarity, and founder of the Schiller Institutes

Dec. 18—If another bit of evidence were needed, the latest EU summit (Dec. 17-18) provided it: This "European Union" is neither a union, nor European. Instead of promoting with one voice the general welfare of the people of Europe, the EU showed itself once again to be a lobby for the bankers and the speculators, who use ever more totalitarian measures to act against the interests of people— people within the EU, as well as the refugees.

On refugee issues, the EU has demonstrated—of course with the exception of the generous aid of many people in Germany and elsewhere—that the oft-cited "European values" don't exist. The "Photo of the Year 2015" chosen by UNICEF, showing the brutal treatment of the refugees on the infamous Balkan Route, is an indelible mark of shame. Of the 160,000 people who, according to the EU's resolution, should have been distributed among various EU member states, only 200 have been accommodated.

UNHCR/B. Sokol

A Syrian refugee camp in Turkey, which is being paid billions of dollars to keep refugees out of Europe.

Death Sentences for Refugees

The deputy Foreign Minister of Greece, Nikos Xydakis, told the *Wiener Zeitung* exactly what it would mean for the security of the EU's borders if they were militarized by an armed Frontex organization: Leading politicians from several EU countries, he said, have repeatedly made the unbelievable and unacceptable demand that the Greek Coast Guard force refugees arriving by boat from Turkey, back into the sea—which would have resulted in their death by drowning. Greece has refused to do this. As a result of this policy, *Spiegel Online* reported, under the headline "Sea of Death," that nowhere in the world did so many migrants die in 2015 as on the external borders of the EU—5085, to be precise.

This same EU, which was able to find trillions of euros in order to "save" the deadbeat banks which had gambled people's money away, has paid Turkey *three billion* euros to stop the refugees from coming to Europe. As Amnesty International has just made public, Turkey—which bears no small responsibility for the refugee crisis due to its support for the terrorist IS,—used this money, among other things, to either deport Syrian refugees back to Syria, or to hold them in prison-like detention camps.

As if this wheeling and dealing weren't abominable enough, according to the *Bild-Zeitung*, at the beginning of the summit the EU Commission knowingly provided the EU heads of state with obviously false counts of the refugees, to justify the massive financial payments to

Turkey. A paper ascribed to Juncker claimed that instead of the level of 52,249 refugees a week, who were arriving at the end of October, only 9,093 per week had come from Turkey in the previous weeks. But, according to the internet site *Politico.eu*, owned by Axel Springer SE, there is an internal paper of the EU Commission which reports that in the week of December 7 to 13, 27,069 refugees from Turkey arrived in Greece alone. Thus, according to *Bild*, Juncker had reduced the number of refugees by approximately a factor of three.

The gentleman has much practice in such deceit, as he confessed in an interview with *Spiegel* back in 1999: "We decide something, then put it in play, and wait a while to see what happens. If there is no huge outcry and no revolt—because most people don't even grasp what has been decided,—then we go further, step by step, until there is no turning back." This practice earned him the nickname "Flunker-Juncker" (Juncker the Deceiver).

And to bar refugees from Africa, the EU has now made two billion euros available—believe it or not!

What the EU has proposed, both earlier and at this recent summit meeting, as the solution to the refugee crisis, is totally bankrupt, morally and politically. The idea that several million refugees from Southwest Asia and Africa should be repelled with gun boats, and that the drowning of thousands and hundreds of thousands must be accepted,—while the EU at the same time carries out a neoliberal economic policy which condemns Africa to the underdevelopment which is the underlying cause of the massive refugee flow—is as far from reality as it is disgusting.

Europeans on the Chopping Block

Such contempt for human life is also expressed toward people within the EU. After four local savings banks in Italy went bankrupt, banks which had encouraged more than 100,000 customers to invest in subordinated bonds, a "bail-in" on the Cyprus model was applied. This wiped out many people's entire savings and deposits, and led a 68-year-old retiree to commit suicide,—which led to a wave of protest. The incident was all the more scandalous, because the big investors had been warned beforehand, and had safely taken out their money, which in some cases ran into the millions.

After the bail-in expropriation of depositors and bank stockholders in cases of insolvency was applied for the first time in March of 2013 in Cyprus, Jeroen

Rijksoverheid/Valerie Kuypers

Bail-in advocate and Euro Group head Jeroen Dijsselbloem, in a picture taken in 2014.

Dijsselbloem, the head of the Euro-Group (Eurozone finance ministers), declared that this would be the blueprint for the entire EU. He has now again affirmed that the application of bail-in is absolutely necessary, and on January 1, 2016 the corresponding guideline, which has meanwhile been approved by all the EU member states, will officially go into effect.

The trans-Atlantic financial crash—which will make the collapse of Lehman Brothers and AIG in September of 2008 look like a joyride in comparison—is already in full swing. Four hedge funds have already gone bust in the United States, because, like the entire shale gas and oil sector, they were entangled in a five-trillion dollar derivatives bubble; the oil price has fallen to under $35 a barrel while their contracts had been concluded on the basis of a price of $80 a barrel or more. Likewise, the bubble in the commercial real estate market—where the entire global crisis of 2007-2008 got its start—has now grown even larger than in the Summer of 2007.

On January 1, Puerto Rico is supposed to pay a billion dollars on its total debt obligation of $72 billion; this is money it doesn't have—and on which, again, hedge funds and banks depend. They are thus threatened with insolvency. In the province of Alberta in western Canada there has been, and still is, a a series of insolvencies in the shale oil sector, which have touched off a wave of suicides among those affected.

The United States' official unemployment rate of 5% is a bad joke. In reality there are more than 100 million people of working age who are not employed—largely because they have given up trying to find work. Forty percent of the employed make less than $15,000 a year—that corresponds to the minimum wage—and half of these make less than $5000 a year. Included in the job statistics are those who work only one day a month.

In reality, the entire trans-Atlantic sector is in the midst of a collapse which is gaining more and more momentum. Faced with indebtedness and derivatives exposure amounting to the trillions, the U.S. Administration and EU have only one card up their sleeves—"quantitative easing," i.e., further money-printing, and the bail-in, i.e. the expropriation of depositors, and bond and stockholders. This can only be described as criminal. The more this crash expands, the more human lives it will cost.

The planned bail-in which Euro Group head Dijsselbloem has just once again defended, is a policy which will cost more lives by far than the gunboat policy of the EU in the Mediterranean. If the goals of the so-called Report of the Five Presidents, announced in July, were to be implemented in full, the EU would become a full-fledged totalitarian dicta-torship, serving the bankers' interests.[1]

There is a solution. The entire trans-Atlantic region must immediately put through the package of measures with which U.S. President Franklin D. Roosevelt began, in 1933, to get the United States out of the Great Depression. The Glass-Steagall bank separation system must shut down the casino economy of Wall Street and the City of London, and in its place a credit system must be introduced in the tradition of Alexander Hamilton, FDR, and the policy of the German *Kreditanstalt für Wiederaufbau* (Bank for Reconstruction) after World War II, which put into effect long-term investments in the reconstruction of the real economy.

With this policy we can rebuild the economies of Southern Europe and the Balkans, which have been destroyed by the policies of the Troika. We must replace

---

1. The report, "Completing Europe's Economic and Monetary Union," is known as the Report of the Five Presidents. It was prepared by the President of the European Commission, Jean-Claude Juncker, in close cooperation with Donald Tusk, Jeroen Dijsselbloem, Mario Draghi, and Martin Schulz, respectively the presidents of the European Council, the Euro-Group (Eurozone finance ministers), the European Central Bank, and the European Parliament.

There Is Life After the Euro!

Program for an Economic Miracle in Southern Europe, the Mediterranean Region, and Africa

AN **EIR** SPECIAL REPORT

CONTENTS
Introduction by Helga Zepp-LaRouche
Greece, and a Marshall Plan for the Mediterranean Basin
Spain: Bridge to African Development
The Rebirth of Italy's Mezzogiorno

Africa Pass
The Transaqua Project
North Africa: The Blue Revolution
What Europe Can Learn from Argentina
A German Economic Miracle for Europe

http://www.larouchepub.com/special_report/2012/spec_rpt_program_medit.pdf

self-destructive geopolitics with a new paradigm, whereby the international community works together to develop all of Southwest Asia and Africa.

The obvious approach for doing that is the extension of China's New Silk Road and the proposal of the Schiller Institute for expanding this program into the World Land-Bridge to bring peoples together, and thus overcoming the conditions which are the fundamental source of the refugee crisis.

In this way we would not only put our own economy back on the track of economic growth, but even more importantly, we would can stop the collapse into total barbarism and win back our humanity.

'Austerity Suicides' In Italy Hit 560

by Liliana Gorini

Dec. 26—The case of Luigino D'Angelo, the 68-year-old pensioner from Civitavecchia, near Rome, who committed suicide Nov. 28 after he lost all of his savings to the bailed-in Banca Etruria, has become world-famous. What called special attention to this tragedy was that, before committing suicide, D'Angelo had written a letter, found weeks later, accusing his bank of stealing all his savings, after having assured him that the "subordinated bonds" he had bought were safe.

But Luigino D'Angelo was by no means the first victim of the economic crisis, and of the austerity imposed on Italy by the European Union, nor will he be the last, unless Italy decides to leave the European Union and go for Glass-Steagall, as Movisol, LaRouche's movement in Italy, has been proposing since 2009.

Between 2012 and 2015 there were in total 560 "economic suicides" in Italy, as the Italian press calls them, people who committed suicide for economic reasons. They were mostly entrepreneurs in northern Italy, who had built a family business, a medium-sized company, which was the pride of their lives, and were ashamed of being forced to shut it down, either because they could not pay their tax debt, or could not get any more bank credit. In the first six months of 2015 alone, there were 121 suicides.

In 2012 there were even cases of self-immolation by individuals overwhelmed by their economic difficulties.

Most of the suicides have taken place in the Northeast of Italy, the former industrial triangle which used to be the richest area economically and socially. Twenty-five percent of the suicides occurred here. The second highest concentration (20%) was in the impoverished South. Forty-five percent of suicides have been by entrepreneurs and managers of companies, but 42% of them were among the unemployed.

Among the unemployed, 12.4% were younger than 34 years.

ISTAT, the National Institute of Statistics in Rome, stopped counting the suicides in 2012, claiming that it is too difficult to keep track of them. But ISTAT did release other relevant data. By August of 2015 the number of deaths in Italy increased by 11.3%, an increase in mortality which had not been registered since the last war.

"It is a shocking number," wrote Prof. Gian Carlo Blangiardo on the demographic website Neodemos. "We have to go back to 1943, or even earlier than that, to the years between 1915 and 1918, in order to find a similar pattern." ISTAT does not explain this dramatic increase in deaths.

Russia Today

Italian students march against austerity in Rome on Oct. 9, 2015.

It Goes to the Soul of the People

Below are edited excerpts from Lyndon LaRouche's webcast discussion with the LaRouche PAC Policy Committee of December 21. Links to the referenced Brooklyn Handel performance and the Manhattan Handel performance . Here is the program for the Brooklyn performance and the Manhattan performance.

Matthew Ogden: Good afternoon. It's December 21st, 2015; my name is Matthew Ogden, and you're joining us for our LaRouche PAC Policy Committee weekly Monday afternoon discussion. I'm joined via video by Bill Roberts, who is currently in New Jersey; Dave Christie, from Seattle, Washington; Kesha Rogers, from Houston, Texas; Michael Steger from San Francisco, California; and Rachel Brinkley, who I understand is back in Boston, from her weekend in Manhattan. And here in the studio, I'm joined by Diane Sare and Megan Beets. The three of us had the chance to participate in a musically victorious weekend in New York City; as you can see, we're also joined by Lyndon LaRouche. So, go ahead, Lyn.

Lyndon LaRouche: OK. First of all, to start

Schiller Institute

The performance of Handel's Messiah at the Sacred Hearts of Jesus & Mary/Saint Stephen R.C. Church in Brooklyn, New York, Dec. 19, 2015.

with, just to put my own voice on this view, we really have achieved an access to our purpose which we've not had before. This celebration, in both these two events, these Saturday and Sunday events, has redefined the whole way we look at things, in terms of what the population is. And we're going to find out that,—as from some of our people who are coming from California, and so forth, who are quite familiar with this business—they probably have picked up something about this over the course of the weekend. And they will be drawn in, as from California, they will be drawn into the effect of what happened in Manhattan in these two performances. And that has changed the character of the United States. And you have certain parts of the states in the United States which really, from this standpoint, are not exactly the best stuff you want.

And so, I think we have established a movement, an action, which is going to lead us into a sudden and good change in the perspective of the United States as a whole. And we need it right now, because the question is—we're on the edge of the destruction of United States. Most of the people who are officials in the United States, the government officials, are failures. Most of them are failures. And they had this new Congressional decision a couple of days ago [the Omnibus spending bill which went against all necessary actions such as Glass-Steagall], and it was garbage, absolute garbage.

So therefore, what we did in terms of the music operation,—what we did actually broke open a new way of thinking about the United States. And what we organized in Manhattan, and we're sure our members in California and elsewhere, will understand that,—this was a great victory for our cause. And I think we probably should take off from that point, at that point of the discussion, because there's so much to be discussed.

Human Beings Are Better

Diane Sare: This has been a process over the arc of the last year, or a little bit more than a year, since your decision to move the organization into Manhattan. And then what became clear, in the wake of various events occurring about a year ago, such as the St. Louis, the Eric Garner murder: is that you have, especially under Obama, an attempt to really divide the population and to bestialize the population. And people want better than that.

So what occurred a year ago when we did the *Messiah* sing-along, is people said, "Can't you organize a chorus in New York?," which we began to do, and it definitely has evolved in fits and starts. We had rehearsals in one of the schools that was kind enough to let us use space, and you'd have four people show up, and wonder if this was going to move forward.

And now the chorus we had in these two performances was seventy-five people, which included guests, like some of the people on this show today, but also a group of people, some of whom had never really sung before, some of whom had sung in other choruses; and it came together. And what we did was, in Brooklyn, we organized the neighborhood around this church, which has a very strong history in the Italian-American community, and the Italian singing community. And it really resonated on the question of the Verdi tuning.

And then in Manhattan also, the question of the Verdi tuning was a big deal, but it was a slightly different dynamic, and a slightly different audience. So between the two places, each of them had somewhere around 500 in attendance; both churches were completely packed.

We had dozens of people who have signed up to join the chorus in the next phase of this process. And I think this was a very decisive demonstration of the scientific tuning. There were many, many comments at both performances, of people saying, "I could really hear the difference. I can hear what you're talking about." One person writing in, said, "I like the way the chorus was in different groups." They don't have another way to express it, but they're hearing now the differentiation of the voices in the chorus, in a way that they had not heard before.

And when you looked out at the audience in the Brooklyn one, there was a young girl, maybe seven or eight years old, seated in the front row, and I kept looking at her because she was just transfixed, completely motionless, just *watching* this.

At any rate, it's a great potential. Everybody who was involved was very happy. There are all kinds of invitations. People have other things they want the chorus to do. I think, again, it is this question that human beings are better. We are not animals. And when people see that expressed demonstrably, then there's a resonance with that, and they want to be part of it.

Ogden: The event was co-sponsored by the Schiller Institute, which has also been involved in hosting a number of very high-level, important conferences in Manhattan over the period of the last year, and the Foundation for the Revival of Classical Culture, and I thought its Executive Director, Lynn Yen, made some very important remarks before the concert yesterday, saying the original performance of Handel's *Messiah* was not in London, but in Dublin. And it was a benefit for widows and orphans who were suffering from extreme poverty at that time.

But just as urgently, the performance of the *Messiah* today is to address, as you said, the gross injustices that are being committed against the American people as of now. I think, Lyn, you're absolutely correct that this is a very timely and very urgent intervention into the population of New York, because, as you've said, Manhattan is the leverage point around which we're going to change the policy of the entire country.

And we're right on the verge of a total meltdown of Wall Street, with the deadline of January 1st, with the Puerto Rico default that's set to occur. The bail-in laws that are going to go into effect in Europe have already been enacted in the case of Italy. You have the suicides that are occurring there. Also the collapse of the shale oil bubble in the Alberta tar sands. All of this, the junk bond meltdown, all of this is conspiring, all at once, to create a situation which is going to be far worse in its effect than the crash of 2007 and 2008.

We are Not Animals

LaRouche: I think we have to view the fact that we do have an implicit leverage that we can hit these people with, on this issue. And what we've done in Manhattan here, already in the two days, we have made a blow out there, which really threatens to shake up the whole thing.

The problem is the Congress decided to make some new laws, and these are *stupid* laws. And they should go back to kindergarten, and learn to become adult people; not adulterated, but adult.

Ogden: Good policy.

LaRouche: No, this is what we're getting. And we really have to translate the effect of this, in terms beyond what we ourselves enjoyed. We have to realize that there's something there which is going to have to influence the nation. And therefore, we're going to take the Manhattan standpoint, that kind of standpoint, and use that as a weapon to change the attitude of the nation.

We have problems. In the course of time, there was a degeneration in the quality of the members of the society.

And so therefore, what we can probably do is infect certain parts of the United States outside the Manhattan area, and so forth, and bring this thing back into a different view. Just use the authority, and the fact that we're better, saying, "you don't want the El Cheapo, do you?"

Kesha Rogers: Well, just take the Dark Age degeneracy of Obama, and his promoting of "Star Wars,"— complete Dark Age conditions. This is the degenerate culture that we are contrasting with a total revolution of beauty. We were talking about this earlier this morning, myself and another organizer, that we need to replace the degeneracy of Obama and the British Empire, what he represents, with more Handel's *Messiah*s, and more beauty that can be propagated throughout the entire nation. And the effects of this concert are already rever-

An etching of George Frideric Handel (extreme right) conducting his Messiah *in the 1740s.*

berating in many ways people wouldn't even imagine. So I think, definitely, those who weren't there can look forward to more. And those who were participating in it may not even know what they have unleashed, that's gotten around far and wide already. And I think there's definitely more to come.

LaRouche: Well, absolutely. That's why I want to put my own point in on my own account on this.

Look, what happens is, when you're talking about this kind of music: it is not a kind of music as such. It's much more than a kind of music. What this is, it goes to the soul of the people.

You take the case of the Italian business. Now the Italian school,—which is as we've known it, was actually a definition of music which was superior to most of the French varieties. Going "eunhh" is not really exactly a good way of getting this spirit of mankind across. And you have other kinds of problems with this case.

But the fact is, when we get into this kind of approach, and particularly on music, on music as such, that you actually define a power which exceeds anything from any alternative approach. When music is placed in this way, as by the Italian school, in the Classical Italian school, and you see what the attempt to do the same thing in Germany was, even though that stumbled back and forth; and the French "unnhh" is just too much to swallow most of the time. But what happens when you get the music done, as was done in the two cases this weekend,—what happens, is you actually inspire people. They don't always know what they're inspired by, but they experience the fact that they participate in it. And that is the principle of science.

And you know the old saying about Bertrand Russell,—you take Bertrand Russell out and you burn him, downwind, into the bad end of the Solar System, or something like that. But now the point is, that when you do something like that, this kind of music is not just good music. This is a matter of principle, which is a human principle, specifically human principle; and it's the ability to develop that kind of principle, understanding that kind of principle, as opposed to so-called popular music. Popular music, popular entertainment, actually degenerates the quality of the mind of the members of the society.

And therefore, you have to say, "what is this about the Italian school as such, which is a very specific thing?" And you have a German school; and you actually have a Russian one, even though it got mutilated by some of the things that happened along the process.

Ogden: But it was largely influenced by the Italian school.

This is Our Weapon

LaRouche: As *all* of it was done on the basis of the Italian school. Brahms, the same thing.

So that this concept of music is not something as "entertainment." That's silly, that's stupid. Right? The question is, if you don't have music of that kind, your mind is defective. Your opinions are defective; you become an "El Stupido." And it's true, because when people are ignorant, they are ignorant! And if you don't have a voice which can be placed, in the sense of placing the voice properly, on different kinds of approximation,—degrees of approximation of perfection,—without that, you don't have a human identity.

You have a bar-hall entertainment kind of thing. You know, you go to some place in Texas, deep in Texas, in the more evil places in Texas of the earlier times, and that's what you get. And they're out there shooting each other, and things of that sort.

But the point is, this implication has to be emphasized. And it's now been demonstrated by these two events on Saturday and Sunday, and therefore this is the weapon with which to build what we must do for man-kind as a whole. Because it's in tune; you've got Russian factors; China is developing, emerging, so forth; all these kinds of things.

And therefore, when you take these principles of the human mind,—not the words, not the language, not the accounting or whatever. But that's what is here. That's what's crucial, and that's our weapon. That was our weapon in Manhattan, in two days, with the preparation that led into that. And so you prepare something for a period of about a year, just approximately about a year, as we did here. And you come to a point where you have this large audience in Manhattan. And they're enthusiastic.

And the characteristics of their approach are great, whereas the average person, outside that circle, is actually very mentally ill. That is, they have mental illnesses by virtue of the inability to place their voice in the right way. And just think of the placing of the voice issue, and think about the different kinds of accents that you find in the United States in different locations. And you look at those accents and you say, "Now, I don't want to be critical of the accents, but this one stinks." And therefore, "we ought to cancel that one out."

These differences in languages in terms of the Classical languages so-called, all depend upon the adaptation to a quality of representation of the human mind. And every kind of speech has to be checked for that kind of thing. Not just song, but voice itself. And the quality of the mind, the quality of the opinion of mind, and Bertrand Russell understood that perfectly.

Ogden: Handel's *Messiah* is a very fascinating piece in that regard, because it is in English; it's one of the few great masterpieces in English. But bringing the Italian school to bear on how this piece is sung and performed, and with the Verdi tuning, transformed the effect of the English language to convey something which is profound, you know, in a Shakespearian kind of format.

LaRouche: Ah! Excellent! That's a most appropriate reference, because that's what Shakespeare did, in his own way.

Ogden: Right.

LaRouche: And this is exactly what we need. And what we have to do is, essentially, achieve that, bring that into reality for more people. So don't worry about this or that. If you bring in a powerful voice of mankind like this, you will resonate throughout the planet.

A Human Sound

Megan Beets: That was reflected in one of the audience members who commented at the intermission that he was blown away by the chorus, because it had a "human sound," which is the only word he could use to describe, I think, what several people here have discussed: the clarity of the chorus; the use of the language to access something which is not accessible by the words, but which we were able to achieve with the Italian method and the placement of the voices, that the conductor John Sigerson was able to bring about.

And I think it resonates with something which came up in your dialogue with the Manhattan group on Saturday which you just referred to, which is that mankind is not an animal; mankind is the only species which can access a principle of universality, something which rises above the individual manifestations of mankind as such, but which the mind of man can actually reach toward. And the examples you gave were Kepler, whose mind was actually able to access the discovery of a principle of universality, which is the extension of the universe as he knew it. And that's the process in the footsteps that we're following in now.

LaRouche: Try Brunelleschi.

Beets: Yes, him too.

LaRouche: That's the key. Brunelleschi had an intellectual capability which

George Friderich Handel studied music in Italy from 1706 to 1710, before moving to England.

Ricardo André Frantz
Italy's Musical Renaissance: From Luca della Robbia's Cantoria (choir loft), originally in the Florence Cathedral.

was beyond any person in his own lifetime. There were some people earlier who made great achievements, but they didn't last very long; they'd last one generation, and that is exactly the point. And therefore, what we have to emphasize is that. We have to emphasize that there's a human, a truly human quality of behavior which corresponds, like magic.

It's the way to do it properly, as opposed to being foolish, or dumb or stupid. And this is the thing that happened in the school system. What happened is, my experience even then, was that the school system tended to produce degeneration, intellectual degeneration. Grunting and all these kinds of things and stupid kinds of things; the emphasis on sports—now I'm not against sports, but the emphasis on sports in education is really bastardizing. And that's the point.

So therefore, I think we just emphasize this, the way we can do it with the music. If you can place the musical voice correctly, then you can lead into what we want to get to in terms of what the human mind is capable of recognizing as the identity of the human being. As opposed to being a grunter, like a pig out there waiting to be porked.

There's actually a principle of humanity which governs the human mind. But when you talk about people, you get into a problem, because you try to interpret what people say they believe in. And that does not give you a solution. But there *is* in the course of human speech and human development of the human mind, there is a course which is correct, and which does correspond to what the purpose of mankind is. And in most cases, we have characteristics of populations which more or less make people ignorant.

The very kind of language they use, the way they express themselves, defines them as ignorant. Now if they become popular in this form of ignorance, what do you get as the quality of the population?

Or, how do you demoralize people, to induce them to kinds of behavior which do not accord with human speech? In other words, you violate the very principle of what makes human speech, human speech,—and you get into grunting rather than speaking!

And the typical case in today's population, is they tend more to grunt than to speak or to sing. And therefore, the idea of the principle of singing actually, when properly understood, leads toward what the intention of the human mind is. So it's not a question of what we can impose upon the human mind; it's a question of what the human mind can impose upon people, for purposes of creativity, and advancement for science and so forth.

Just take all the people who are educated to teach mathematics. Now, anybody who teaches mathematics has a problem. There's a defect in their mental makeup. Even if they do have a good mental behavior in what they say at times, they also go into other periods where their understanding is not so good. Because they adapt to a practice of speech which is contrary to the intention of human speech, as opposed to what it should be. And we call this intention "music."

And when the music is good, when it's competent, we are happy with the music *per se*, because the music is being tuned to the human intention. And in these other cases, then you get into an area where people run around and say silly kinds of things, and grunt and groan and so forth, and make the pigs blush every time they pass by and speak!

And that's what the problem is. So mankind, by failing to develop the natural intention for mankind's development,—then if you violate that, you cause a destruction in the morality, in the broadest sense of morality, of a human population. Whereas if you perform, in this case, the kind of thing we're talking about, the two cases in Manhattan right now immediately,—

what's the point there? What was the effect of what was done in these two choruses?

Ogden: From Brooklyn, right.

We Miseducate Children

LaRouche: And I know I'm resonating from Manhattan. So the point is, is that when you get into that area, you do find by taking the right music, and the right expressions which are musical-like events,—that these things define the morality of the human individual. The morals of the human individual are located in the way they think; and the way they think is in terms of the proper musical thing, what we would recognize as—and the Italian case is an excellent example of the case we're focusing on as that particular point.

And Brunelleschi is not inconsistent with that. He was the greatest genius in terms of science in his whole lifetime. He was a miraculous power in his own lifetime. Others had to learn from that; they were sitting around there being geniuses, and "bluh-buh-buh," you know!—not so good. But his genius was great! And that's what it is, what we call the true scientific genius has the same quality. They don't like to do things which they know aren't human.

And so, I think the problem is that now we can take this, and Manhattan is a better choice, shall we say, than some other places. And therefore, what you have to do,—the music is the principle. When the music is defined properly, the music is the principle, instead of mathematics. It's mathematics that kills music, that kills the mind.

Beets: If you can stimulate children to experience the human mind through music, and they begin to get a joy, the kind of joy they experience with feeling the mind, that's what they can carry over and apply in all other areas of study,—scientific areas in the classroom and so forth. But the most efficient and powerful, and maybe the only successful way to stimulate that, is through Classical musical composition and things related to it.

LaRouche: You have to get rid of mathematics. If you start to think in mathematical terms, you become stupid.

Beets: Yes. With mathematics, you build a wall between yourself and knowledge of any principle.

LaRouche: So therefore, you use the human mind, follow the human mind with poetry, with Classical poetry, and Classical poetry in different expressions,—*all* this corresponds to this same requirement. And what happens is, we miseducate people,—we miseducate children. We make whole parts of the population dead minds, because of that. Mathematics is the greatest threat to the human mind that could possibly exist.

Schiller Institute

Mezzo-soprano Mary Phillips singing the Messiah at the Dec. 20, 2015 performance at the Unitarian Church of All Souls, Manhattan, New York.

Ogden: You made that point very clearly I think in the discussion on Saturday in Manhattan, about what is the result of a Hamiltonian credit policy? What you earn after investing that credit into an economy dominated by national banking, like Hamilton did, is you earn increased productivity. You don't necessarily earn more money; that's not what you're attempting to earn. What you're earning, is an increased productive power of your labor force.

Manhattan Is Superior

LaRouche: Which is called the principle of truth. What is the natural principle of human truth? Because the human mind operates on the basis of the human mind, not on mathematics. That's where the problem comes—with the attempt to induce habits in children and others, which are not in accord with this kind of conception of the human mind. That's why the Italian,—and we refer to the Italian as such. It's so important because it is tuned, primarily; it is tuned. It is tuned more or less appropriately and that's what made the thing so good.

And the problem is, when you think of mathematics and try to interpret everything in terms of mathematics, you are an idiot. You may not know you're an idiot, because you couldn't find the answer to why you were actually an idiot.

And that's the point: The human mind operates in a different way than any of these pedagogues understands today. So therefore, when you introduce what we're talking about, these two events, in Manhattan and in Brooklyn,—what you're doing is you're actually going to the music, which is not just music *per se*; it's the way the human mind functions competently. And when you're in resonance with the human mind, you should not indulge in anything which is not resonant with the human mind.

But you have to understand what the human mind is. And most children today don't have any idea what the human mind is; they're destroyed. Why do you think all these youth, in California and so forth, are degenerates? It was done to them, by taking the music away from them! And this is the issue. And that's what this is: We won a battle on two days successively. And we did it just about right. I heard enough of it to know it was just about right.

And that particular selection was particularly appropriate historically: It goes to Bach! It goes directly to Bach.

Ogden: Yes. A little known fact about Handel's

Messiah is that Benjamin Franklin, when he was in London, attended a performance of the *Messiah*, and he writes about it in his memoirs or in his diaries, it had such an effect on him.

LaRouche: Well, this is what the whole thing is about. And now I think we're at the point we can just openly say, "This is it. Here are two cases right now; two cases, they demonstrate the point." And we got 1,000 people in total up there, attending. Now, that hasn't been done for a very long time. And so therefore, Manhattan and its associated functions *has* a superiority over the other guys!

Schiller Institute

John Sigerson, Music Director of the Schiller Institute, conducting the Messiah at the Dec. 20 performance in Manhattan.

Michael Steger: I think that listening to the discussion and the nature of the concerts, if you put it in the context of what, Lyn, you laid out prior to both of the concerts on Saturday afternoon, in the discussion with the participants in Manhattan: Over the next few weeks, we're facing a moment where our nation and Western civilization are going to have to make a decision of what course of action, what course of direction, we're going to take. And you see that what's been so lost in this process, is this quality of human mind.

There seems to be almost an involuntary instinct for progress within human society, but it's not a conscious sense of it. You know, I'd say that Plato was almost intrinsically Italian. Because he had this sense, and he knew the difference. He knew that you could have agreement,—we get agreements all the time. Obama's not good; Glass-Steagall yeah, we'll need it, I'll sign the bill,—but you see no action taken! You see no action; it just seems as if they agree with the opinion.

And what this musical tradition, what you get from Dante, or you know, Shakespeare, who took much from Boccaccio, this Italian school which fought against a Dark Age for *action*, not for "agreement" that this Dark Age sucks! That's clear! The question is action to change it, action to uplift it! That's true knowledge, that's Plato's idea.

LaRouche: That's absolutely true. For me, that Saturday for our organization, our members who were involved, that's exactly what happened. They all agreed; the agreement was not a formal one, the agreement was an implicit one.

And that's what we actually got by doing that,—in cleaning up the problems of the California organization, we touched *into* that! And you find that all these members who were there speaking in response to me, they *all* agreed! And that was the secret.[1]

So we had a meeting of members, and we know more or less the categories in which they fit,—their professional categories and so forth,—and they *all* agreed. They saw this as a solution. And that's what I mean.

And we're doing the same thing with music in California, and here also.

That's exactly the key to this thing, and somehow we've got to get that idea delivered to people. And what's happened—these two events on Saturday and Sunday—has now established a proof, not just the experience but a proof of something, and it worked.

Steger: I think we've started a Renaissance.

---

1. A 50-minute colloquy on Dec. 12 between Lyndon LaRouche and a group of activists in Alameda County in northern California.

Brunelleschi and Shakespeare

LaRouche: Why not? Well, of course, and I think the Saturday event which I addressed there in California, fits that perfectly. They responded exactly to that issue. All we have to do,—we get the Congress shaped up, and we have the making of what we have to do.

Ogden: And Manhattan remains the center of it. I mean, the two points that you've been making, are, we need Glass-Steagall to shut down Wall Street, immediately. The fact that hasn't happened yet is a crime, and it's setting up the United States and the rest of the trans-Atlantic system for a blowout of unprecedented proportions.

And we need to defeat the 9/11 principle. What happened on 9/11 was *never* disclosed to the American people in terms of the Saudi role. The suppression of the 28 pages has created the environment where you've had two successive Presidential administrations that have been increasingly working against the interests of their own population. And the fact that you now have the emergence of a total Dark Age situation in the Middle East and North Africa as a result of successive regime-change overthrowings of these governments, sovereign governments in that region,—that is a consequence of the fact that the truth was never told about what really was behind the events of 9/11.

So both of these needs have as their central focal point, a very concerted intervention into the population of New York City.

LaRouche: It's more, it goes more deeply than that. You see the all of the facts of history: "Where'd Hitler come from?" Well, Hitler came from the British. That's where he came from. He was a British agent, and that became very clear.

So the point is that evil, and—well, I would say, algebra, algebra is a sinful thing. It's terrible. We could give a grade in algebra as a sin.

No, it's true! The point is art,—Shakespeare's conception of art is very appropriate, if you understand Shakespeare. These are the kinds of things I used to have great fun with, in Shakespeare; because he never placed himself as being the hero. He placed himself as looking at man, and looking at what is ridiculous in human behavior, at what should *not* be ridiculous. And he was good at that! And that's the whole history of modern art.

And Brunelleschi is actually one of the most important figures in this whole process. His creativity was absolutely astonishing to everybody around him! I worked with some Italians in science in that area, and we had a meeting where we had the leader of this group and his sister, and we were doing the research on this.

And at a certain point on this business, I went back to Germany and they stayed in Italy; so both of us, me and him, both had a certain experience: I was on the train going back to Germany, he was there sitting in Italy. And about the same time that I was midway back to Germany, it came to me, "Oh my God, this is the solution!" I called them, "Oh yes, we just discovered the solution, too."

Ogden: You're talking about the time when discussion around the maintenance of Brunelleschi's Dome was taking place?

LaRouche: No, no, this was earlier, but the same kind of thing was going on! And it was essentially,—Brunelleschi was absolutely unique. Without him, there would have been *no* Renaissance, none! It was his influence on the way ideas were dealt with, where Brunelleschi was actually the *author* of the principle on which the Renaissance developed. And there were precedents in this area. But you had what happened to Jeanne d'Arc: Jeanne d'Arc was murdered, and she was almost exterminated, totally.

So the point was, the question is, you need figures of mind who have a *concept*. Now, Jeanne d'Arc had a concept. There's no question about that. But she was in a setting which was not trustworthy; now if her friend [the future Louis XI] had become the King, if Jeanne d'Arc had lived until he came into his role, then she would not have been murdered. But these kinds of things can come into play. And these are the kinds of things which you have to look into in history. And the main thing is to understand that music is the basis of everything.

Ogden: Yes.

LaRouche: It is! It is, actually. Because you're actually relying on a device of the human mind which is not the conventional practice today.

So we have now made an experience *with* history. We've not made history, we've made an experience with history this weekend.

'If You are Human, You Should Sing!'

by Susan Bowen

Dec. 26—Under the baton of Maestro John Sigerson, the Schiller Institute New York City Chorus and Orchestra last week demonstrated the quality of creativity necessary to reverse the crisis of civilization facing our nation and the world.

At the beautiful Sacred Hearts of Jesus and Mary/St. Stephens Roman Catholic Church in Brooklyn, New York on Saturday evening, Dec. 19, 2015, the first of two unique presentations of the often-performed *Messiah*, by George Frederic Handel (1684-1759) was sung in the Italian bel canto style, at the Verdi tuning (middle C at 256 Hertz, A at 432). The Brooklyn concert was dedicated to the Principle of the Sanctity of Human Life, and was opened with a welcome and prayer by the Rev. Msgr. Guy Massie.

The soloists in both concerts were Rosa D'Imperio, soprano; Mary Phillips, mezzosoprano; Everett Suttle, tenor; and Jay Baylon, bass-baritone. Maestro Sigerson was particularly attentive to Handel's intention, his words, his voicing, and his message, thus gripping the audience with a much richer and more profound *Messiah* than they had heard before.

On Sunday, Dec. 20, young students, teachers, music lovers, church members, neighbors, musicians, people who got a flyer on the street, civic and political activists, and curious individuals who had never heard a classical concert, filled Manhattan's All Souls Unitarian Church to capacity to hear the performance. Lynn Yen, Executive Director of the Foundation for the Revival of Classical Culture, which co-sponsored the event, welcomed the standing-room-only audience, who came to hear Handel's *Messiah* speak to them of Peace on Earth and Good Will toward Mankind.

Schiller Institute

John Sigerson conducting the Schiller Institute chorus in the Mozart Requiem in Boston, Jan. 19, 2014.

Conceived as an intervention against the violence, the wars, and the lack of Classical education that permeate our depressed economy today, these beautiful concerts of the "Manhattan project" succeeded beyond expectation. Many who came signed up to join the choir, the Foundation, and the Schiller Institute movement, and the New York City landscape has been transformed as a result of the performances at these two historic churches.

Read the programs and learn more.

• Program for Messiah Performance on December 19 in Brooklyn.

• Program for Messiah Performance on December 20 in Manhattan.

Interview with John Sigerson

I interviewed John Sigerson, Music Director of the Schiller Institute, on Dec 26, a few days after he conducted the extraordinary performances of Handel's Messiah *in Brooklyn and Manhattan. I was fortunate to participate in the chorus in these historic events, and I can report that throughout the rehearsals and right up through the performance, John's constant refrain to his choir, and also to the orchestra, was that we were never to just "sing the notes"! He insisted that we sing the music, the ideas, and communicate what Handel had intended in his Messiah. From all accounts by those who heard the live concerts, this sublime mission was accomplished. We discuss that in the interview below.*

Bowen: You conducted Handel's *Messiah* in New York. This is one of the most often-performed works in the United States, and yet these two performances were unique. To start out, can you talk about why the Schiller Institute Chorus and orchestra perform at the "Verdi" tuning (where Middle C is at or near 256 Hz, and the "A" is no higher than 432 Hz)?

John Sigerson: All the great Classical composers, from the time of Brunelleschi and Guillaume Dufay in the Italian Golden Renaissance up through Johannes Brahms, understood that music, both vocal and instrumental, must never stray from the primacy of the beautiful, well-placed human singing voice. During the mid-1980s, in the course of wide-ranging discussions about the scientific discoveries of Nicholas of Cusa and Johannes Kepler, combined with discussions about Classical poetry and German *Lieder*, Lyndon LaRouche decided that the time was over-ripe to return to a tuning which is in harmony with the underlying principles of the human singing voice, and specifically with the way the human voice is organized into registers.

These registers are, in fact, of the same nature as the orbits of the planets in our Solar System as investigated by Kepler. And just as those orbits aren't accidental, neither are the vocal registers! And the tuning that works best with these registers, happens to locate Middle C at, or around, 256 cycles per second.

We quickly discovered that indeed, this was the tuning demanded by Verdi, in opposition to those who sought to raise the pitch to arbitrarily higher values, supposedly in order to make instruments sound more brilliant. It was also the tuning preferred by Mozart, Beethoven, and many others.

So we started a campaign to return to the natural tuning, and enlisted the enthusiastic support of a number of the world's greatest singers of the time, including the baritone Piero Cappuccilli, who, in a video you can see on the Internet, conclusively demonstrated the superiority of the Verdi tuning. And then Norbert Brainin, the first violinist of the famous Amadeus Quartet and already a longtime friend of Lyndon LaRouche, demonstrated that his Omobono Stradivarius also works best at C=256 Hz.

So, things went on from there. We tuned our pianos down, shattering the myth held by many that it would destroy the instrument. I trained our chorus at the lower pitch, and found that it was much easier to train beginners, and that advanced singers felt that they could finally spread their wings vocally, so to speak. I co-authored a book on the principles of registration and tuning, and I also collaborated with the tenor Carlo Bergonzi on a demonstration at Carnegie Hall in New York City, where he warned that unless we returned to the Verdi tuning, the days of great "Verdi voices" would never return.

Bowen: Great opera singers, like those you mention, Cappuccilli and Bergonzi, are *bel canto* singers, as are most professional soloists. But your choral singers also train in "bel canto" singing, the method of especially of Italian opera singers. The Schiller Institute New York City chorus is a Community chorus, open to everyone, so the participants are not professional singers. Can everyone learn to sing in a chorus?

Sigerson: Well, if you're human, and your voice is not seriously damaged in some way, you should sing, and strive to sing Classical music, since it's the best way to educate your emotions along the lines discussed by Friedrich Schiller in his letters on the aesthetic education of man. And what better way to sing than with a chorus of people dedicated not just to singing for self-gratification or entertainment, but to the same moral purpose as Schiller's? That's why I've never been in favor of excluding anyone who wants to join our chorus, even if they may have serious vocal limitations, whether those be of the physiological sort, or of the psychological sort such as so-called "tone-matching."

Of course, we're fortunate enough to have a core of experienced singers who can help the beginners along. We also encourage chorus members to attend smaller

Choristers celebrating the Fall of the Berlin Wall with Beethoven's Choral Symphony on Christmas Day 1989.

sessions with others of the same voice type, so that we can create as much of a conservatory-type spirit as possible, given people's other life responsibilities.

Retuning All the Instruments

Bowen: Handel's *Messiah* is written in English, and quotes from Bible passages, so it should be quite intelligible to an American audience. Following the performances, audience members in these concerts said that not only were these presentations intelligible, but, in fact, seemed to be much more "alive," as if speaking directly to them. Why was that? Is that why the words and the phrasing were so articulated? Can you give an example?

Sigerson: Americans' speaking habits nowadays have degenerated way below what they were, say, 100 years ago or more, and when they sing in their own language today, they tend to bring in their bad habits more than if they were singing in a foreign language such as German, Italian, or Latin. One of those bad habits is speaking in a mechanical way, where each syllable is spat out like machine-gun bullets, in a rapid monotone.

For example: People will say, and sing "For the glory of the Lord" in such a way that they put just as much emphasis on "the" and "of the" as they do on "glory" and "Lord." So, they may be singing the notes correctly, and even with decent vocal production, but the effect is totally mechanical and unpoetic.

Therefore, in my rehearsals of *Messiah*, I've been insisting on a natural delivery that is in keeping with the natural tuning and placement. To continue my example, not only do you want to de-emphasize "the" and "of the," but you also want to lengthen the "gl-" of "glory" and especially the "L-" of "Lord."

I could go on and on with more examples, but it wouldn't make much sense in print. Just come to one of my rehearsals and you'll understand.

Bowen: Regarding the orchestra. I understand that string players can easily modify the tuning of their instruments by simply adjusting the tension on the strings. Wind and brass players are much more limited in their ability to modify the tuning. How did you approach this question of tuning the instruments to the Verdi pitch?

Sigerson: We're still in the process of getting all the instruments in shape to play at the Verdi tuning. As you said, the tuning of the strings is generally not a problem, though it's sometimes not easy for a string player to quickly make the adjustment.

As for the winds and brass, we demonstrated in Boston in early January 2014, with our performance of Mozart's *Requiem* in commemoration of John F. Kennedy's assassination, that some instruments can be made to play at the lower pitch in the hands of a highly-trained professional. The clarinets, for instance. Also, for last weekend's performances, we had Matthew Ogden playing a modern Heckel bassoon with a custom bocal (the mouthpiece where the double reed is mounted) which Heckel kindly manufactured for us. It worked perfectly!

There are certain instruments, though, which just can't be modified like that, but which need a complete re-design. The oboes, for instance: As it stands, we have to rely on replicas of historical oboes such as were played during Mozart and Beethoven's time, but we really need modern oboes specifically designed for the Verdi tuning. Perhaps the Chinese will be able to help us out on that.

Bowen: Lyndon LaRouche, who developed the idea of the "Manhattan project" originally, discussed the success of the process on the Policy Committee Show on Monday.

He emphasized the importance of the placing the voice properly:

> …It's now been demonstrated by these two events on Saturday and Sunday, and therefore, this is the weapon in which to build what we must do for mankind as a whole. Because it's in tune; you've got Russian factors; China is developing, emerging, so forth; all these kinds of things. And therefore, when you take these principles of the human mind, not the words, not the language, not the accounting or whatever. But that's what is here. That's what's crucial, and that's our weapon. Our weapon in Manhattan, in two days, with the preparation that led into that....

Stuart Lewis

Norbert Brainin in a rehearsal for his Dec. 2, 1988 concert in Washington, D.C., in honor of Lyndon LaRouche. He is accompanied at the piano by Gunter Ludwig.

In that same discussion, he said:

> These differences in languages in terms of the Classical languages so-called, all depend upon the adaptation to a quality of representation of the human mind. And every kind of speech has to be checked for that kind of thing. Not just song, but voice itself. And the quality of the mind, the quality of the opinion of mind, and Bertrand Russell understood that perfectly.

How does this apply to what you worked on in the *Messiah,* and with the music work generally? Why would Bertrand Russell be so upset with how these concerts communicated Handel's idea? What is meant by voice placement, if it's not just making the sound, and how does music resonate in the mind?

Closer to the Creator

Sigerson: Well, no man, and no chorus, is an island! It's important to understand that our Manhattan Chorus is part of our overall "Manhattan project" which intends to pull not only New York City, but the entire nation and the world from an otherwise unimaginable abyss. The rehearsals with the chorus are informed by that intention in ways that are more unspoken than spoken, especially since rehearsal time is short, and I have to concentrate on mastering the music, and not on lectures. The placement of which Lyndon speaks, flows precisely from this.

One aspect of this which is terribly important, though, is the tempo. Unlike time-beaters such as Arturo Toscanini, I agree with Wilhelm Furtwängler that the tempo must never be totally fixed, and that it must organically move with the flow of ideas. This generally means broader tempos than those which Bertrand Russell would probably have preferred, such as the quick tempos introduced by Russell's contemporary Sir Robert Beecham in his 1927 recording of the *Messiah* which I heard the other day.

Bowen: Diane Sare, the founder and director of the Schiller Institute New York City Community Chorus, reported tremendous interest in the Schiller Institute Chorus, with many wishing to join, others wanting to collaborate, and many wanting to learn about the tuning. And as a result of these performances and the ongoing musical interventions, there also are numerous invitations for the Schiller Institute chorus to perform at the Verdi tuning at various venues. So as this choral movement grows throughout New York City, do you have other thoughts you would like to share with our national and international readers?

Sigerson: Working with the Manhattan Chorus challenges me and all the singers alike to rise to the level of the poet of Percy Bysshe Shelley's mind, for whom music, poetry, science, economics, and political leadership are governed by the same principle of the ever-increasing perfection of mankind. This brings us ever closer to the Creative Principle itself, or the Creator, if you will.

As I pointed out to some of my associates the other day, our intention is therefore not to put on "professional" performances, but rather to go way beyond that, in the same way that Furtwängler did with his performances of Schubert's Ninth Symphony, Beethoven's Ninth Symphony, and Brahms's Fourth Symphony, among others. Study Furtwängler, and you'll begin to grasp what I'm talking about.

Bowen: Thank you, John.

Sbowen@SchillerInstitute.org

The Call to Arms of The Manhattan Project

by Dennis Speed

I am astounded that I found myself agreeing with Lyndon LaRouche. Handel's Messiah *need not be performed in a tuning system with "C"=246 hertz, and "A" no higher than 432 hertz, instead of A at 440 or higher, but I am listening to the* Messiah *at the Unitarian Church at 80th and Lexington in New York, being conducted by John Sigerson, and sponsored by the Schiller Institute, with Helga and Lyndon LaRouche's encouragement ... this is an extraordinarily fine performance, fitting within the natural vocal ranges of the soloists and chorus, and with a very strong orchestral support.*

Dec. 28—As in the earlier experience of Boston's January 2014 Schiller Institute performance of Mozart's *Requiem*—a 50th anniversary recognition and re-enactment of Jacqueline Kennedy's musical request immediately following the assassination of her husband, President John F. Kennedy—disbelievers in the legitimacy of the idea of "proper tuning"—as well as the urgent necessity of the views of Lyndon LaRouche—were grudgingly converted, again, in New York City over December 19 and 20. In Brooklyn on Saturday, and Manhattan on Sunday, a truthful performance of Handel's great *Messiah* was rendered by a small orchestra and by a 75-person chorus, plus soloists, that performed at the "Verdi tuning" of middle C equal to 256 cycles per second. (The A is tuned to a range of 427-432 cps.) This is nearly a quarter-tone or more lower than the tuning presently in use at several of the most prestigious opera houses in the United States and Europe. Higher tuning creates a distortion in the music as originally composed by Mozart, Beethoven, Bach, and other of the Classical composers.

The New York Schiller Institute Community Chorus was expressly created to reverse this arbitrary but intentional distortion, and to instigate a revolt against the dumbing-down of the over one million students in the nation's largest school system—and of American culture and civilization as a whole—by beginning with the central subject of music.

Brunelleschi Again

The just under one thousand persons who directly participated in those two concerts were presented not with a mere musical performance, but with a new stan-

On the podium at the Schiller Institute's May 1994 conference "For a Marian Anderson National Conservatory of Music Movement": Noted African-American musicians bass-baritone William Warfield (left), vocal coach and accompanist Sylvia Olden Lee, and tenor George Shirley (right).

dard for American citizenship. Music, and musical literacy and practice, including public performance by the citizenry, is as much a right and a responsibility of free government as is the bearing of arms to defend one's nation.

The proper tuning allows for the natural placement of the human singing voice, which is the "first among all instruments" and the central starting point for all forms of instrumental composition as well. This, in turn, returns us to the musical setting, and therefore, the intention of the Classical composer, assuming the performers and conductor now submit to the power contained "behind" and "above" the composition's text. Now, great music becomes intelligible and reproducible, including to all who have the desire to know it and to participate in it.

An Italian singer and vocal coach who has closely watched the process of organizing that the "proper tuning movement" directed by the Manhattan Project is carrying out, has referred to it by the name *Risorgimento*, the name associated with the Italian fight for independence in the which the composer Giuseppe Verdi was intimately involved, both as a musician and as a member of parliament. Not only does a "dark age" in Classical music exist in America today, according to this singer. Other singers and performers who have been active in the school system in Italy report that, since approximately 1975, the earlier Bel Canto singing tradition of that nation has also been largely ripped apart.

A trans-Atlantic collaboration to re-establish Bel Canto is therefore now under discussion, also involving collaboration with other organizations such as the Foundation for the Revival of Classical Culture, which sponsored the Sunday concert at All Souls Unitarian Church. Immediately, the goal of the Manhattan Project is the creation of a 1500-person chorus, the majority of whose members would make up the basis of a city-wide movement to establish an international core that wields Classical musical composition in the same way that Martin Luther King's civil rights movement wielded the African-American Spiritual in the 1960s.

To that latter end, choral directors Diane Sare and John Sigerson have insisted that their singers familiarize themselves with the conductor Wilhelm Furtwängler, and particularly his performance of Schubert's Ninth Symphony. Sare has had the choral members sing the instrumental parts of the opening of that symphony as an *a capella* exercise, not merely to emphasize the vocal quality of that composition, but to also reveal the vocal-contrapuntal compositional method that Schubert advanced for that symphony's purpose.

Composer Johann Sebastian Bach, and particularly his first of what are called the *Two-Voiced Inventions,* has been similarly studied with vocalization, in the one-hour solfège class that precedes a Saturday dialogue with Lyndon LaRouche. It was LaRouche who inspired and conceptualized the 1980s campaign to re-establish the Verdi tuning, culminating in the work known as *A Manual on the Rudiments of Tuning and Registration*, published in 1992 by the Schiller Institute. *Messiah* conductor John Sigerson was one of the co-authors of that manual.

LaRouche has now urged that his Manhattan Project colleagues take up study of the Florentine scientist Filippo Brunelleschi (1377-1446), to really get at the *purpose* of music. And while many know that there was for hundreds of years an emphasis by the cathedral builders of Europe on musical proportion in architecture (such as the completion by Abbot Suger of the choir of the St. Denis Basilica in France in 1135-1144), Brunelleschi's musical discoveries in the dynamic application of the art of proportion went far beyond anything that had been achieved up to that time.

While Brunelleschi is most famous for his creation of the Dome at Florence, recent discussion of his work on the small Pazzi Chapel was the occasion for comment by LaRouche.

> Helga and I walked into this chapel, and the whole thing was like a living creature. You're just in there. You were seized by this little chapel; it gripped you. You couldn't get free of it! You have to get out of it in order to see something else which was there, but it was like the whole thing was a living process! And that was the quality of [Brunelleschi's] work. Everything he did was absolutely unique, and highly variegated and so forth. And that's what we have to look in ourselves for, in order to understand what we must do in dealing with the crisis which comes on us immediately right now.

Rooted in Deeper Science

The choral Manhattan Project will break new ground in the United States as LaRouche has proposed. There is an earlier New York City precedent. The 1890s project of Czech composer Antonín Dvořák (The *New*

World Symphony), his American sponsor Jeanette Thurber, and, indirectly, Johannes Brahms in Europe, the National Conservatory of Music, was revived by the Schiller Institute in 1992, the 100th anniversary of Dvořák's arrived in America.

Dvořák was eloquent on the purpose of this project. The Conservatory project was not only not supported by the United States Congress; it was also undermined by those who objected to the notion that America's Classical compositions would emanate from African American Spirituals as their primary base. Only the yet-to-be-born New Orleans jazz was to be permitted, or other non-Classical practices, as African Americans were excluded summarily from schools and concert halls once the National Conservatory was effectively undermined by the mid-1890s. Dvořák was forced to return to Europe.

Today's situation is far worse than that which Dvořák faced, because of the comparable destruction of the entire practice of Classical musical practice since the 1960s, in particular. So is the Presidency far worse. So is the Congress, and perhaps, also, the population. As Martin Luther King said, however, in his April 3, 1968 speech: "But I know, somehow, that only when it is dark enough, can you see the stars." The worst of situations submit to and may be overcome by the power of poetry, as Percy Shelley attests.

The methods brought to bear by the Manhattan Project are rooted in a deeper science than that of the earlier cultural attempts. For example, in Europe the work of Brunelleschi, Nicholas of Cusa, and Johannes Kepler was succeeded by the foundation of the well-tempered system of musical composition by J.S. Bach. This is crucial for any "music student" to know and to master, but is generally unavailable in any music conservatory. By focusing on the Bel Canto voice placement principle, from the advanced standpoint of the compositions of the Classical period from Bach through Brahms, Dvořák, and Verdi, and the conducting principles advanced by Wilhelm Furtwängler, it is possible to introduce tens of thousands of New York

New York Historical Society

Frederick Douglass (1818-1895), a forceful advocate for Classical culture.

citizens, in the short term, to a new, human view of language once characteristic of American oratory and public speech.

Consider, for example, this sentence taken, essentially arbitrarily, from an 1851 Rochester, New York public address by former slave Frederick Douglass, whose every conscious moment was spent at that time clearly delineating the basis for the freedom of all men as clearly enunciated in the Constitution of the United States:

When I speak of *such* men, I can find no more appropriate language than the words of our Savior to the Scribes and Pharisees; and if any here deem the language I have already used harsh, or denunciatory, I commend to them the burning words of our Savior, applied eighteen hundred years ago to the same class of men as those who are now standing in the way of the slave's redemption: "*Woe* unto you, Scribes, Pharisees, hypocrites, for ye pay tithe of mint, and anise and cumin, and have omitted the weightier matters of the law, judgement, mercy, and faith."

These Douglass speeches were virtually never written. They were declaimed indoors and outdoors, in all sorts of halls, schools, and churches, and with no amplification. Can anyone seriously imagine any of the Presidential candidates, or any of the too-prevalent semiliterate street orators, or television personalities, or talking heads, or Fox News screechers, or late-night television talk show hosts, or talk radio semi-pundits, speaking this way?

What was the music of speech that Douglass heard, and what is the music that they hear? What music is Donald Trump hearing? What music is Barack Obama hearing? What music is the Congress playing to drown out the sound of the Constitution being murdered every Tuesday by Barack Obama's kill sessions?

Only by introducing a different practice of musical participation, including performance, in the population as a whole, in strategic parts of the United States, can this otherwise terminal civilizational condition be reversed. This is an essential pre-condition to re-establish the capacity of our society to elicit the moral fitness to survive from an otherwise doomed citizenry, now exterminating itself at an accelerating rate through drug and alcohol abuse, suicide, and various forms of non-lethal menticide, both self-inflicted and institutionally encouraged.

The defense of the republic cannot be successfully accomplished by the illiterate and semi-literate, no matter how good their announced intentions. In today's United States, where the past two Presidential administrations have operated with the express intent of reducing the population of the United States itself through various forms of foreign and domestic warfare and economic deprivation, and where the sitting President holds a Nero-like and publicly acknowledged "kill session" every Tuesday,—is it any wonder that a mass shooting/killing occurs now every day?

EIRNS/Stuart Lewis

A quartet of LaRouche movement members playing in August of 1985. From left: Seth Taylor, Nancy Shavin, Renee Sigerson, and David Shavin.

Aldous Huxley was Wrong

In 1962, in a speech given at the University in California at Berkeley, after he had returned from a Santa Barbara Conference at the Center for the Study of Democratic Institutions, Aldous Huxley infamously remarked:

> There will be, in the next generation or so, a pharmacological method of making people love their servitude, and producing dictatorship without tears, so to speak, producing a kind of painless concentration camp for entire societies, so that people will in fact have their liberties taken away from them, but will rather enjoy it, because they will be distracted from any desire to rebel by propaganda or brainwashing, or brainwashing enhanced by pharmacological methods. And this seems to be the final revolution.

In 1974, political associates of Lyndon LaRouche who had been victims of drug-induced brainwashing, sometimes combined with physical assault, countered the effects of that brainwashing through intensive listening to the late Beethoven string quartets. These compositions acted as a particularly effective emotional mooring point, more powerful in their expression of human creativity and triumph than the then-crude, opposing methods popularly utilized by police agencies of 40 years ago. Such pedagogical exercises, properly supervised, can in fact reverse the sorts of effects that Huxley terms final.

Yes, great damage has been done, but if people gain the courage to wipe out Wall Street and its false conception of the value of human life, then that act itself will re-establish the sanity of the society as a whole. But from where will come the courage to do this?

This is where the truly revolutionary role of Classical music composition and performance comes in. People are not, in the final analysis animals, unless they intend to be. Today, simply reintroducing Classical musical principles will have a salutary effect, but that is not enough. To save civilization, it is essential to exemplify the future which is worth saving. That future is not "programmatic." It is not "pragmatic." It is not a "good, empty campaign slogan" like "Hope and Change." It must ring emotionally true, and *be* true at the same time.

As we enter January and a new phase of cultural crisis, forces associated with Lyndon LaRouche's Manhattan Project have vowed, as their New Year's resolution, to supply the American population with the *ganas*—the desire (or, less delicately, the "testicular fortitude") to "take arms against a sea of troubles, and, by opposing, end them."

The arms to be taken up, are not bullet-firing semi-automatic weapons, nor apocryphal "Star Wars" light-sabers. They are the same weapons that the great Italian patriot and artist Giuseppe Verdi forged and wielded in his battle for a sovereign, single nation of Italy, a "Risorgimento," which would successfully conclude a battle that the Florentine poet and statesman Dante Alighieri had waged and died in the service of, more than 500 years before Verdi's work. LaRouche has specifically identified the Italian Bel Canto vocal training approach as the urgently required basis for teaching Americans what LaRouche refers to as voice placement. This is not esoteric or unintelligible—rather, it is an attack on unintelligibility.

The grunting that passes for public speech, most luridly on display in the political campaign screeches of Donald Trump, or the even more offensive Chris Christie, should reveal to the listener the mind only of the criminally insane. This is apparently, however, not the case; many Americans seem to no longer be able to hear how simply crazy these people, and their present President, are.

Has America been driven morally tone deaf by the noise now called popular music? What is the relationship between what Americans choose to listen to, and the political candidates that they tolerate listening to? Sixteen years of depressive dumbing-down, first by the "country and western" braying of the not merely illiterate, but anti-literate George Bush, followed by the "smooth jazz" patter of Barack Obama's constantly contentless statements, was recently rudely and thankfully interrupted by Vladimir Putin at the September United Nations 70th Anniversary session. Americans and the rest of the world gratefully witnessed, by comparison, two opposing speeches, containing two opposing conceptions of world leadership. One was human speech; the other was not.

Silent No Longer

The purpose of the Manhattan choral project is to equip each citizen who volunteers to reverse the demise

Lynn Yen, Executive Director of the Foundation for the Revival of Classical Culture, makes opening remarks at the Dec. 20 performance of the Messiah *at the All Souls Unitarian Church in Manhattan.*

of civilization and humanity that is presently the sure outcome of the downward spiral that Barack Obama's United States is leading the world into, with the moral weapons to accomplish that mission. Our power in this, is the capacity of reason in others. This capacity must, however, be awakened as an emotional disposition to act, not merely as a contemplative consideration of "what might be the right thing to do." We are past the time for that.

In welcoming the audience for the Sunday *Messiah* performance at All Souls Church, Lynn Yen, founder of the Foundation for the Revival of Classical Culture, concluded her remarks by saying:

> You cannot convert a man, woman or nation by killing him, her, or it. "You have not converted a man merely because you have silenced him." Handel's *Messiah*, Beethoven's Ninth Symphony, Mozart's *Requiem*, and other works are the most powerful "weapons of mass instruction" ever devised in Western civilization. When will we learn that this, not the gun or the bomb, is the true way to help change humanity for the better? The answer is, we will learn it only when so many young people around the planet, starting in places like the United States, understand the true dignity of mankind, because they have heard and performed it in this music; you will

then be unable to silence them any longer, because they will have for the first time heard and been moved by the sound of their own singular voice.

Antonín Dvořák's Manhattan Project

by Dennis Speed

Dec 28—During his 1892-1895 sojourn in America, composer Antonín Dvořák brought to our nation, and to New York City in particular, the compositional methods of Classical music, represented at the highest level then in Europe by Dvořák's friend, sponsor, collaborator, and fellow artist Johannes Brahms. Dvořák composed his Ninth Symphony "From The New World" and his famous Cello Concerto at his home on East 17th Street, located a few blocks from the Conservatory.

His friendship and musical collaboration with the African-American composer, arranger, and instrumentalist Harry Burleigh, violinist Will Marion Cook, and others resulted in the initial highlighting of the African-American Spiritual as the basis for the creation of a new American school of composition. Burleigh's singing of the Spirituals for Dvořák, along with their discussions about the fight against slavery and its eradication in the United States, was the artistic basis for Dvořák's composition of the famous Second Movement of his Ninth Symphony, centered around an original theme often wrongly presumed to be an African-American Spiritual.

Dvořák's insistence that a "great and noble" American culture must be based on the work of the poor, and the opportunities that they might be provided through such institutions as the National Conservatory of Music, would not have been welcome among the increasingly pro-British "aristocrats" of New York City, nor the racists of the E.H. Harriman family's Eugenics Records Office, established in Cold Spring Harbor in 1904, less than 10 years after Dvořák returned to Europe.

Though the National Conservatory would remain open until 1945, it was suppressed almost immediately. Stravinsky's 1913 *The Rite of Spring* would replace Dvořák's symphony as the "Classical music" that would most affect—or infect—Twentieth Century America.

A letter to the Editor of the *New York Herald* written by Dvořák, and published May 29, 1893:

I was deeply interested in last Sunday's *Herald,* for the writer struck a note that should be sounded throughout America. It is my opinion that I found a sure foundation in the Negro melodies for a new national school of music, and my observations have already convinced me that the young musicians of this country need only intelligent directions, serious application, and a reasonable amount of public support and applause to create a new musical school in America. This is not a sudden discovery on my part. The light has gradually dawned on me.

The new American school of music must strike its roots deeply into its own soil. There is no longer any reason why young Americans who have talent should go to Europe for their education. It is a waste of money and puts off the coming day when the Western world will be in music, as in many others, independent of other lands. In the National Conservatory of Music, founded and presided over by Mrs. Jeannette Thurber, is provided as good a school as can be found elsewhere. The masters are competent in the highest sense and the spirit of the institution is absolutely catholic. A fresh proof of the breadth of purpose involved iin the conservatory is the fact that it has been opened without limit or reservation to the Negro race.

I find good talent here, and I am convinced that when the youth of the country realize that it is better to now stay at home than to go abroad we shall discover genius, for many who have talent but cannot undertake a foreign residence will be encouraged to pursue their studies here. It is to the poor that I turn for musical greatness. The poor work hard; they study seriously. Rich people are apt to apply themselves lightly to music, and to abandon the painful toil to which every strong musician must submit without complaint and without rest. Poverty is no barrier to one endowed by nature with musical talent. It is a spur. It keeps the mind loyal to the end. It stimulates the student to great efforts.

If in my own career I have achieved a measure of success and reward it is to some extent due to the fact I was the son of poor parents and was reared in an atmosphere of struggle and endeavor. Broadly speaking the Bohemians are a nation of peasants. My first musical education I got from my schoolmaster, a man of good ability and much earnestness. He taught me to play the violin. Afterward I traveled with him and we made our living together. Then I spent two years at the organ school in Prague. From that time on I had to study for myself. It is impossible for me to speak without emotion of the strains and sorrow that came upon me in the long and bitter years that followed. Looking back at that time, I can hardly understand how I endured the privations and labor of my youth.

Could I have had in my earlier days the advantages, freely offered in such a school as the National Conservatory of Music, I might have been spared many of my hardest trials and have accomplished much more. Not that I was unable to produce music, but that I had not technique enough to express all that was in me. I had ideas but I could not utter them perfectly.

There is a great opportunity for musicians in America and it will increase when grand opera sung in English is more firmly established, with public or private assistance. At the present time this country also needs the materials for orchestral work. The dearth of good native performers on reeds and brass instruments is marked. Everyone wants to sing or play the piano, violin or violoncello. Nobody seems to realize the importance of good cornetists, trombonists, clarinetists, flutists, trumpeters and the like. In Bohemia applicants for admission to the Conservatory are assigned to instruments according to the necessities of the time. Of course nearly every young musician wants to play the violin, but to encourage that tendency would be to undermine the orchestral system and leave composers without the means of properly presenting their works.

I do not agree with those that say that the air here is not good for vocalists. The American voice has a character of its own. It is quite different from the European voice, just as the English voice is different from the German and Italian. Singers like Lloyd and M'Guckin have an entirely different vocal quality from that of German singers and members of the Latin race. The American voice is unlike anything else, quite unlike the English voice. I do not speak of method or style, but of the natural quality, the timbre of the voice. I have noticed this difference ever since I have been in New

Czech composer Antonín Dvořák (far right), with his family and friends in New York City in 1893.

York. The American voice is good; it pleases me very much.

Those who think that music is not latent in the American will discover their error before long. I only complain that the American musician is not serious enough in applying himself to the work he must do before he is qualified to enter upon a public career. I have always to remind my most promising pupils of the necessity of work. Work! work! work! to the very end.

The country is full of melody, original, sympathetic and varying in mood, color and character to suit every phase of composition. It is a rich field. America can have great and noble music of her own, growing out of the very soil and partaking of its nature—the natural voice of a free and vigorous race.

This proves to me that there is such a thing as nationality in music, in the sense that it may take on the character of its locality. It now rests with the young musicians of this country and with the patrons of music to say how soon the American school of music is to be developed. A good beginning has been made in New York. Honor to those who will help to increase and broaden the work.

—Antonín Dvořák

Sweet Power of Song

Sweet power of song! That canst impart,
To lowland swain or mountaineers,
A gladness thrilling through the heart,
A joy so tender and so dear:
Sweet power!

—Irish folksong,
elevated to musical poetry
by Ludwig van Beethoven

Dec 26—If one is preparing to fight a war, or even a major battle, it would be a fatal mistake to underestimate either the strength of one's adversary or the actual nature of the battlefield. Such is the challenge we face today. In truth, American culture, as well as that of the nations of the European Union, is careening further and further into a Dark Age, an age no less perverse, degraded, and irrational than that of the 6th or 7th centuries, or the years following the Black Death of the Fourteenth Century. It is not pessimistic to recognize the reality and the enormity of the problem confronting us. The truly fatal mistake would be to ignore this current state of affairs, to go about one's business with misguided blind optimism, or to assume that the population will respond rationally to proposed solutions for dealing with the current global breakdown crisis.

Given the existing state of the American population, particularly those between the ages of twenty and forty, it must be understood that reasoned dialogue and rational proposals to solve the urgent problems confronting society will fall on deaf ears, the deaf ears of a people which has been degraded, day-in and day-out, to the depths of what is portrayed in the *Satyricon* of Gaius Petronius.

To win the battle ahead, in this year of 2016, something greater, something far more profound, something which gets to the essence of the human identity is required to ignite a spark within the hearts and minds of the people.

Following on the heels of the two historic performances of Handel's *Messiah*, presented by the Schiller Institute's New York City Community Chorus on Dec. 19th and 20th, 2015, *Executive Intelligence Review* is pleased to present the following package of articles by Theodore Andromidas, Marcia Baker, and Susan Bowen. These articles, taken as a whole, demonstrate that, at an earlier time, it was the power of Classical culture, and the recruitment and participation of ordinary Americans in that culture, especially in Classical musical composition and performance, which played a vital role in transforming growing numbers of people into better citizens, better human beings. In his article, Ted Andromidas makes the point that, in a certain, specific way, it was the participation of millions of Americans in the Federal Music Project which prepared them for the fight to defeat fascism.

The purpose of this package is not to evoke useless nostalgia for the past. Nor is it to present a formula on how to win our present fight. Rather, think of it this way. Most Americans today will not fight for anything truly important. They will argue, they will bitch and complain, but they won't stand up to authority and fight for the future of humanity. They are afraid. They lack courage. If you want people to fight, maybe, first, you should get them to stand up … and sing. Stand up and participate in a choral process. Perhaps hearing their own voices, raised in song as part of a Classical chorus celebrating that which is best in human nature, will give them the confidence and moral courage to stand up and fight for a better future.

Franklin Roosevelt's Cultural Vision

by Theodore Andromidas

> The American Dream ... was the promise not only of economic and social justice but also of cultural enrichment.
> —Franklin Roosevelt, 1938

Dec. 27—With the *Compromise of 1877*[1] that withdrew all U.S. troops from the South, and the Supreme Court's decision in the *Civil Rights Case* of 1883,[2] the United States would begin a retreat from the great moral vision for which so many had fought and died just 20 years earlier. This retreat became a virtual rout with the murder of President McKinley in 1901 at the hands of a British Imperial assassin. The United States would not begin to emerge from an ever-deepening dark age for decades. This moral and intellectual descent, led by "the most evil man of the Twentieth Century," Bertrand Russell,[3] threatened to end the United States as the "last great experiment for promoting human happiness."[4]

Franklin D. Roosevelt Presidential Library

Before the New Deal: A one-room school in Alabama, circa 1935.

Educating into a Dark Age

A review of the changes in the American education system following the *Compromise of 1877* provides a good look at the cultural decline of the United States into what would have become, as in Europe and elsewhere, a new dark age of fascism and war.

By 1880, we find enrollment rates for public school education for the later years of the Nineteenth Century and the early years of the Twentieth, in a precipitous decline. The number of young people enrolled in school remained relatively low in the last third of the Nineteenth Century. In fact, the rate of student enrollment in America's schools in 1900 was almost exactly the same rate of enrollment as in 1840. And, although rates fluctuated, in general, only half of all 5- to 18-year-olds were enrolled in school.[5]

Rates for males and females were roughly similar throughout the period, but rates for African Americans were much lower than for whites. Prior to the emancipation of Southern blacks, school enrollment for blacks was largely limited to a small number in Northern states. Following the Civil War, the enrollment for blacks rose rapidly from 10% in 1870 to 34% in 1880.

However, in the ensuing years, leading into the Great Depression, there was essentially no change in the enrollment rate for blacks, while the rate for whites actually fell. This situation would not change until the

---

1. Reconstruction ended following the Compromise of 1877 between the Northern and Southern political elites. In exchange for deciding the contested presidential election of 1876 in favor of Rutherford B. Hayes, supported by Northern states, over his opponent, Samuel J. Tilden, the compromise called for the withdrawal of Northern troops from the South.

2. The Court held that Congress lacked the constitutional authority under the enforcement provisions of the Fourteenth Amendment to outlaw racial discrimination by private individuals and organizations, rather than state and local governments.

3. "The Incompetence of Twentieth Century Science Education" by Lyndon H. LaRouche, Jr, *Executive Intelligence Review,* April 4, 2014.

4. George Washington, January 9th, 1790.

5. U.S. Department of Commerce, Bureau of the Census. *Current Population Reports*, Series P-20, Historical Statistics of the United States, Colonial Times to 1970.

New Deal. The overall enrollment rates for 5- to 18-year-olds rose from 51% in 1900 to 75% in 1940. The difference in the white and black enrollment rates narrowed from 23 points in 1900 to seven points in 1940, again, in great part, due to the programs of the Franklin Roosevelt Administration.[6]

Education in the Southern tier of the United States suffered terribly during the pre-Roosevelt years. Fewer than 5% of the teachers in this region had college training; more than 60% had no definite professional training of any kind. Although the average annual salary for female teachers during the 1870-1900 period was about $300, average salaries in the South for the same period actually dropped from $175 to $159. Not only were salaries low, but in some cases payment was uncertain. In South Carolina in the 1880s, teachers routinely received vouchers on payday instead of a check. It was considered a progressive step when teachers were paid (much later) the face value of those vouchers rather than a reduced amount.

While illiteracy ranged from 30 to 45% of the total population in the Southern half of the nation (three times that of other areas of the country), only one Southern pupil out of ten who enrolled in school reached the fifth grade, and only one in seventy reached the eighth grade. Poorly equipped teachers worked with almost no supervision, merely "keeping school," as it was referred to at the time. Each small, isolated school was left to itself as county superintendents' jobs routinely went to incompetents as reward for political service; no qualifications were legally prescribed for any positions. The State Superintendent in South Carolina in 1900 reported that "Each district has as poor schools as its people will tolerate, and in some districts anything will be tolerated." Rural schoolhouses in the South during the 1880s and 1890s were valued at less than $100 each.

Alabama's educational system in 1930 was much like the entire Southern tier of the nation. In the early 1900s, education in Alabama still suffered from short school terms, low funding, and racism. In one county, for instance, the average length of the school year was 72 days for white students and only 34 days for African-American students. The value of the typical schoolhouse for whites was $40,000, in contrast to the average black schoolhouse valued at only $1,000. The average annual salary for white male teachers was $863 and for white female teachers $422, whereas African-American male teachers earned $480, and black women teachers just $140.[7]

'New Deal for the American People'

Such was the state of so much of the nation when, on March 4, 1933, Franklin Delano Roosevelt assumed the Presidency. He found a country, not just in the depths of decades-long economic decline and then financial collapse, but a country descending, with the rest of the world, into a new dark age. Roosevelt, who was elected overwhelmingly, had promised a "New Deal for the American people," and worked quickly on an unprecedented number of reforms addressing the catastrophic effects of the Great Depression. Together with his "brain trust," a group of university scholars and progressive activists, Roosevelt sought the best course of action for the struggling nation. A desperate Congress gave him *carte blanche* and rubber-stamped his proposals in order to expedite the reforms. During the first 100 days of his Presidency, a seemingly never-ending stream of bills was passed, and the Congress worked quickly to relieve poverty, reduce unemployment, and speed economic recovery.

Many of these programs are still familiar to us today, such as the Civilian Conservation Corps (CCC), which put three million young men to work within months. We also know that programs like the CCC helped begin the process of taking these young people out of illiteracy and the degradation which had defined the lives of so many since the death of McKinley, a degradation from which they would eventually emerge to rebuild the nation and, perhaps without knowing it, be prepared for the war against fascism.

Through his New Deal, administered by the Works Progress Administration (WPA), Roosevelt would initiate the greatest period of infrastructure building of any nation in the history of humanity.

It was the WPA, directed by his close friend and trusted associate Harry Hopkins, that administered the rebuilding of the United States through infrastructure projects for roads, bridges, schools, courthouses, hospitals, waterworks, and post offices. It also initiated the construction of many other projects, including museums, parks, community centers, zoos, botanical gardens, audi-

---

6. Truman Pierce. *White and Negro Schools in the South: An Analysis of Biracial Education* (Englewood Cliffs, N.J.: Prentice-Hall, 1955), pp.17-42.

7. "Public Education in the Early 20th Century," Gordon Harvey, Jacksonville State University, in *Encyclopedia of Alabama*.

toriums, waterfronts, city halls, and university unions, many of which are still in use today. The infrastructure projects initiated and overseen by the WPA included 40,000 new and 85,000 improved buildings.

We must emphasize here that one of its most far-reaching projects was the creation and expansion of educational and cultural infrastructure: 5,900 new school buildings were built; a total of more than 2,170 additions were made to existing school buildings; an additional 31,000 school buildings were renovated or modernized. Library facilities were improved and expanded, and 1,000 new library buildings were built. Primary and secondary school enrollment rates increased dramatically, and by 1940 illiteracy had been substantially reduced.

One of thousands of posters circulated by the WPA for music education across the United States.

The Federal Project Number One

Roosevelt understood that if he were to succeed in returning the American people to the mission for which the nation had been created, more than just "economic relief" and job training was required. For this purpose, **The Federal Project Number One,** known as "Federal One," for short, was created in 1935 to extend the economic relief, and protection, of the New Deal to artists, actors, writers, and musicians. Many of these men and women had refused to sign on to New Deal relief programs for fear of irrevocably damaging their artistic performance capabilities. The relief programs used manual labor almost exclusively. Imagine if the great Amadeus Quartet or some other group of performers or artists had been forced to dig ditches. Any accident to their hands or feet or eyes could well have ended their careers forever.

Roosevelt also knew, as the future was to demonstrate, that this program could and would provide a great double benefit to the American people. Not only would these legions of unemployed artists be put back to work, but their creations would enrich the minds of a population that had been morally and intellectually devastated by the previous 40 years of cultural and economic decay, which would end in what became known as the Great Depression.

"Federal One" was to become a powerful instrument with which to infuse great Classical art and culture into the daily lives of millions of broken and demoralized Americans. Three years after the establishment of "Federal Project Number One," President Franklin Roosevelt wrote to his friend, the journalist Hendrik Willem Van Loon, on January 4, 1938, "I too, have a dream—to show people in the out of the way places, some of whom are not only in small villages but in corners of New York City—something they cannot get from between the covers of books, *some real paintings and prints and etchings and some real music.*"[8]

Below we will give a brief overview of only one program of Federal One, the Federal Music Project. Although short-lived, along with most of Federal One, it was a bold and successful attempt at halting the decades-long decline of culture and literacy in the United States through the direct support of music and the arts by the government. This is not an attempt to critique the quality or beauty of all the music performed and produced by the Music Project, or most of the art created by Federal One. Rather, it should be clear to the reader that the Roosevelts, Harry Hopkins, and others, as they were attempting to raise the nation out of decades of despair, not just with jobs, but with art, were also attempting to establish the foundations for an American Renaissance.[9]

The Federal Music Project

"If President Roosevelt had done nothing else but establish the Federal Music Project, that alone would be sufficient to account him great." So declared a southern

---

8. Hendrik Willem van Loon (1882-1944) was a historian and children's writer. Born in the Netherlands, he moved to the United States in 1902.

9. We can get a striking glimpse into some of the intellectual depth of the Federal One programs: The Federal Writers Project provided access to some of the first English translations of Nicholas of Cusa published in the United States. They were published by the California State Library, under the Historic Records Survey of Project of Federal One. One was *De staticis*, by the Famous and Learned C. Cusanus."

California musician during the height of the Great Depression. The newspaper which quoted him at the time, concluded by adding: "...this opinion will be confirmed by thousands of musicians and music lovers."[10]

Holger Cahill, director of the Newark Museum of Art, was appointed in 1935 to direct Federal One. Federal One had five subdivisions: The Federal Music Project, the Federal Art Project, the Federal Theatre Project, the Federal Writers Project, and the Historical Records Survey. Just one year after the five national directors first met in Washington, some 40,000 WPA artists and other cultural workers were employed in projects throughout the United States.

Hopkins personally chose Nikolai Sokoloff to head the Federal Music Project. Sokoloff was a Russian-born, Yale-educated violinist who had made his mark in the Boston Symphony. Just prior to being appointed, Sokoloff had organized and conducted a symphony orchestra in New York. He would direct the project through most of its existence.

During its four year history, from October 1935 to August 1939, the Federal Music Project would sponsor an impressive 275,000 live "performances, programs, and recitals" performed before 147,000,000 people in 43 states and Washington, D.C. The Federal Music Project funded various musical initiatives but primarily focused on music composition, performance, and education. University professors, music educators, and professional musicians were *all* eligible for relief, as long as they were United States citizens.

How far the music of the WPA project eased the distress and bewilderment of the depression must, of course, escape exact evaluation, but the contribution to the morale of multitudes certainly was significant.
—Earl Moore, Federal Music Project
Final Report, 1939

For Sokoloff, and the early leadership of the Federal Music Project, America's music would be a continuation of European classics. His disdain for popular music was unrestrained. The ordinarily reserved Sokoloff did not hesitate to denounce it in rather colorful terms. To one reporter he argued that jazz and swing did not represent popular music at all: "*Popular music* is music that endures through the years, as Handel's *Messiah* and the

---

10. Richard Saunder, *Hollywood Citizens Journal,* June 19, 1931.

stokowski.org
Nikolai Sokoloff, first head of the Federal Music Project, conducting the Cleveland Orchestra in the 1920s.

Fifth Symphony of Beethoven—that's popular music. I'd bet more people today in the world know the Fifth Symphony—and it was written one hundred years ago."

And the national director felt just as strongly about embellishments to performances of symphonic or chamber music: "The clever dance arrangements of Classical airs," he told one meeting of music directors, "are as ludicrous as your lovely grandmother made up to look like a chorus girl."

Yet Sokoloff was committed to the development of a uniquely American Classical music. He agreed with the composer Antonín Dvořák, who 40 years earlier, had attempted to initiate a Renaissance in American music. Sokoloff encouraged American composers to create their own symphonic scores.

He told a southern California newspaper: "I believe very firmly that we should give the good American conductors a chance when there are vacancies in these orchestras, and *I believe we should give plenty of opportunity to American composers of merit.*" Yet, as he warned in the Federal Music Project preliminary report, this "administration has had no intention of fostering incompetence."

The Offerings of the Federal Music Project

Millions of Americans saw orchestras, concert bands, and symphonies on tour throughout their states, some led and performed by local talent. Oklahomans could attend performances of the Oklahoma Federal Symphony in Tulsa; Floridians the Florida Federal Symphony in Tallahassee. An estimated 55,000 saw a federal orchestra perform in Milwaukee. In its final report, the Federal Music Project stated: "Great music under the Federal Music Project was no longer the privilege of the more fortunate of the dwellers in cities"[11]

Before 1933 the nation boasted 19 symphony orchestras; the Project directly created 34 new orchestras and helped in the creation of at least 100 more orchestras across the nation. Classical music had now become the "people's music," available to urban and rural areas alike, to the wealthy and the poor.[12]

In its second report to the Congress, the Federal Music Project gave a detailed report of its activities, stating in part:

In this nation-wide movement, inaugurated when communities recognized an irreparable injury threatened the whole structure of American music, there are enrolled instrumentalists, vocalists, composers, teachers, copyists, arrangers and librarians, tuners and instrument repairers. These are the musicians who faced deterioration of skill, the relaxation of vital energies and waning morale with the loss of employment."[13]

By June 30, 1935, 15,000 musicians were enrolled in the following units:
- 141 symphony and concert orchestras, engaging 5,669
- 77 symphonic, military, and concert bands with 2,793
- 15 chamber music ensembles
- 81 dance, theater, and novelty orchestras ...
- 38 choruses, quartets, and vocal ensembles

Library of Congress

At the heart of the Federal Music Project were thousands of performances either free or at cheap "popular prices." Classical Music was becoming "the people's music."

- 141 teaching projects
- 24 projects for copyists, arrangers, librarians, and binders ...
- two vocal and instrumental soloists' projects
- two tuners' and Instrument repairers' projects
- 11 miscellaneous (coordinating, administrative, and clerical) projects.

In developing the program, the first consideration of the WPA was whether there were needy, unemployed musicians of skill in a community where the music program was to be established. Then there were conferences with local sponsors before the project units were created. Once the project was up and running, a primary objective was to involve the American people and its public and private institutions at all levels. City councils, county and township boards; school districts and boards of education, recreation groups, chambers of commerce, service clubs, fraternal orders, and veteran organizations all enlisted as cooperating sponsors. The National Federation of Music Clubs, with more than 5,000 member bodies in 48 states, was among the first to assume responsibilities of cooperating sponsorship.[14]

As the report also emphasized, the Federal Music Project engaged the leading musicians among America's Classical artists. Again, from the project's report to Congress:

Many among America's most distinguished musicians promptly proffered their services in the new Federal Music Project. They saw in this emergency project not only a wise step to conserve the skills of musicians but the potential building, as well, of a new body of musical appreciation in the nation.

In addition to performing thousands of concerts, offering music classes, organizing the Composers Forum

11. Cited in Robert D. Leighninger, "Cultural Infrastructure: The Legacy of New Deal Public Space," *Journal of Architectural Education* 49, no. 4 (1996), pp. 226-236.

12. Eric Hobsbawm. *Nations and Nationalism since 1790: Programme, Myth, Reality,* 2nd ed. (Melbourne: Cambridge University Press, 1992), pp. 131-62.

13. Nikolai Sokoloff. *The Federal Music Project: Second Preliminary Report Covering Its Scope and Activities During Its First Nine Months* (Washington, DC: U.S. Government Printing Office).

14. Ibid.

Laboratory, and hosting music festivals, Sokoloff and his collaborators asserted that music was socially necessary, and that the project's purpose was to "build music into community life through group participation in enjoyable self-expression, and lay a foundation of cultural interest through music appreciation."

Sokoloff believed that Americans were at the beginning of a great cultural change, one that would replace their "frontier spirit" with a great desire for musical creativity. Until the New Deal, the cultural backwardness and ignorance of many Americans was justified under the myth of the "American pioneer spirit." Roosevelt and Hopkins gave Sokoloff and his collaborators the opportunity to change that.

The project included a broad and ambitious music education program. It provided classes in rural areas and urban neighborhoods, providing music education in all public schools which did not have it. In 1939, an estimated 132,000 children and adults in 27 states received free instruction every week. A Composers Forum Laboratory afforded composers in several major cities the opportunity to hear their work performed with complete instrumentation.

The Index of American Composers paralleled the Design Index, cataloguing 5,500 works by 1,500 composers; WPA ensembles performed every one of these catalogued works. Finally, Music Project workers also served as copyists, arrangers, and librarians, expanding the availability of musical work.

Thirteen thousand professional musicians are giving free concerts for the education and pleasure of millions who never before have known such living music. Suddenly America is becoming musically articulate.

— Works Project Administration pamphlet, 1936

Space does not permit examination of the full scope of the performances provided *free* or at nominal cost, to

Library of Congress

A poster featuring the offerings of the Federal Music Project.

the American people. Here is just a small section of the Federal Music Project's *Second Preliminary Report Covering Its Scope and Activities During Its First Nine Months* to the Congress as authorized by Sokoloff, which is a partial listing from the preliminary report of the number of concerts and audiences from each state:

From the regional directors' reports spanning January 1 to June 3, audience figures for New Jersey alone stood at 2,036,406, exclusive of radio listeners. In New York City between October 10 and June 7, 1,094,642 individuals heard WPA music in concert, opera or other public performances. Attendance figures for California from January 16 to June 29, in 3,952 programs or performances, were 2,291,976, and in Illinois, exclusive of the thousands who heard the orchestras supplied for Federal Theater vaudeville or recreational services, 1,415,619 persons heard 1,947 concerts.

In Grand Rapids, Michigan, attendance for the first six months of the year is listed at 60,575, but this does not embrace the music appreciation and educational programs throughout the public and parochial school systems. By including these, listener figures aggregated 162,000 up to April.

Minnesota audiences between January 1 and June 29 heard 813 programs with attendance of 328,030. WPA concerts in Denver, Colorado Springs and Pueblo registered audience figures of 109,609. Connecticut, with its symphony orchestras in Hartford and Bridgeport, reported listeners numbering 159,347. While Missouri had only two concert project units which played to 3,201 persons in Kansas City, St. Louis and two CCC (Civilian Conservation Corps) camps during January, attendance figures had risen until they numbered 44,636 in the six weeks period between May 1 and June 15. The WPA concert orchestra in Joplin began public performances in April, supplying about 11,000 listeners of a grand total of 118,461 in the State for the first six months of the year.

Pennsylvania attendance figures, between February 1 and June 19, including 537,086 in Philadelphia alone, totaled 1,536,197, and this compilation was made before the Philadelphia 100-piece orchestra and its concert band of ninety men had participated in events in late June before estimated crowds of 50,000.

Concert units in six cities in Ohio were heard by 702,371; in Oregon listeners' figures stand at 80,180 which does not include outdoor concerts in parks; programs in Nebraska between March 1 and June 20, principally in Omaha and Lincoln, were heard by 103,905 persons...."[15]

Music education, as with public performances, was also at the foundation of the Federal Music Project. Again, sections of the project report to Congress demonstrate this:

> The program created by the Federal Music Project for the rehabilitation and retraining of the approximately 1,600 teachers of music now on its rolls has disclosed a vast and unexpected hunger for music among large groups of our people. The classes, over which these WPA teachers preside, enroll today literally hundreds of thousands of persons, divided about equally between adults and children.
>
> These teachers are leading and directing classes for group instruction, both vocal and instrumental; they are presiding at community gatherings for talks and demonstrations on music appreciation, history and theory, and they are serving as conductors, instructors and coaches of choruses, bands and orchestras.

Before the Federal Music Project came into existence, it had been estimated that two-thirds of the 4,000,000 children in the 143,000 rural schools in America were without music instruction in any form. Educators had recognized for a long time that the old methods of teaching music in rural schools had not changed to keep pace with other educational trends. Through the teaching of music on an unprecedented scale, this changed under the WPA:

The activities of the WPA music teachers penetrated into the remotest rural communities. The teachers also were leading large classes in the congested areas of the great cities. In Minnesota, Massachusetts and Oklahoma, teaching programs were set up on state-wide bases.

Beyond the immediate benefits in community organization, social music activities entered into many phases of individual life. Their influence was found in the home, cementing family ties and deepening social interests. A more spacious form of self-expression was gained, and the cooperative spirit expanded in ensemble work. For the musician a new field of opportunity appeared. Scores of letters and statements in the press attested these facts.[16]

Musicians, teachers, and musical scholars across the nation were inspired and remoralized by the Federal Music Project. Dr. James A. Mursell, Associate Professor of Education at Teachers College, Columbia University, wrote:

> I regard the work which is being carried on in New York City by the Music Education Division of the WPA Music Project as a most significant enterprise in both its social and musical implications. A great new constituency has been discovered, eager for serious music study, but untouched ... It is being established that opportunities for music study and musical activities are an important element in the well-being of large numbers of persons. This work is making a remarkable contribution about how music should be taught, and its place in the scheme of human values.[17]

In 1939, the Federal Music Project's budget was cut. This wasn't the only reduction in funding of New Deal programs; many other New Deal projects saw their funding reduced. Congressional support eroded in the late 1930s, and the budget bill that was passed in June 1939 reflected it.

Sokoloff had resigned the previous month amid debate over his and the project's preference for Classical music. The opposition came, in part, from within the

---

15. Ibid.

16. Ibid.
17. Ibid.

National Archives

A class in violin instruction under the WPA Federal Music Project in New York City.

project itself, and was led by Charles Seeger, "folklorist" and father of "folk singer" Pete Seeger. (Charles Seeger's actual role in the Federal Music Project remains unclear to this day.) In 1939, the Federal Music Project was renamed the WPA Music Program. It didn't last long. Many state music projects came to an end with the ending of the WPA on June 30, 1943.

The opposition to the Federal Arts Project—and most New Deal programs—was led by Martin Dies (D-Tex.). Dies was one of the two founding Congressional members of the House Un-American Activities Committee (HUAC) in 1938. The committee began to focus its attention on the Federal Theatre Project, which had become one of the New Deal's most vulnerable creations.

The Federal Theatre Project had created a section called *The Living Newspaper* plays, which became the focal point of most of the controversy. Each play identified a social problem and called for specific solutions. According to Brooks Atkinson, a *New York Times* drama critic, writers were "to shake the living daylights out of a thousand books, reports, newspaper and magazine articles" to create documentaries based on current news stories. *Living Newspapers* were collective efforts in many ways. These plays became the obvious points of attack for the demagogues of Dies' committee.

Despite its short life, Federal One and its projects had an enduring effect on the United States. Despite the victories of demagogues like Martin Dies, the effects of the programs would last for decades to come. With the election of John F. Kennedy in 1960, the nation looked forward to another American Renaissance. Perhaps no President in American history, other than Franklin Roosevelt, celebrated the arts more visibly than John F. Kennedy. Kennedy invited Robert Frost to be the first poet in history to recite at a presidential inauguration—a harbinger of things to come.

A few short months later, Frost would be followed by a performance at the White House of one of the greatest musicians of the century, Pablo Casals. During the presidential campaign of 1960, Casals had become aware of the young candidate John Kennedy, and in 1961 he accepted an invitation to perform at the White House as a symbol of his agreement with President Kennedy's view that "we must regard artistic achievement and action as an integral part of our free society."

This new Renaissance was horribly cut short. The next internationally renowned artist invited to perform at the White House was Elvis Presley, and thus began the descent of the nation, again, into a dark age. It is Lyndon LaRouche's announcement of the Manhattan Project in October 2014, and its intervention into American life with events such as the recent performances of Handel's *Messiah* in New York City, which will trigger another rebirth of American Classical culture.

Author's Postscript

In 1935, the year that the Federal One was established, this author's father had just turned twenty. Like so many children of immigrant parents, he was functionally illiterate, having been forced to drop out of school at age 11 to haul coal in his Manhattan neighborhood, "Hell's Kitchen," to help sustain his family. It was directly, in part, the activities and infrastructure created by Franklin Roosevelt's Federal One which gave him the opportunity to become an artist, an architect, and a lover of great Classical art—not to mention a lover of the music of Verdi and the Italian school. —TA

The Manhattan Project and The Spirituals

by Susan Bowen and Marcia Merry Baker

Dec. 27—The world impact of America's unique musical gift to humanity—the Negro Spiritual—was furthered directly by activities in the strategic venue of Manhattan and environs. There is much to tell, but the essence of the process can be conveyed in brief, by referring to African-American composer and singer Harry T. Burleigh (1866-1949),[1] who figures prominently in the battle for Classical culture in America and internationally, and such follow-on developments as the Hall Johnson Choir in Manhattan (Harlem).

The beauty and merit of the Spirituals—the songs of humanity, arising during the terrible conditions of British imperial oppression in the United States—are, or should be, now widely known. What is important to appreciate further, is the deliberate effort made to continue this beauty and potential through Classical performance and composition, a critical part of which took place in New York City. It was there, also, that counter-efforts were concentrated, aimed at degrading the cultural identity of the entire nation, by enemies of America and mankind. In that regard, the pivotal events took place in the 1890s.

By this time, certain fundamental measures were underway after the Civil War, to preserve and extend knowledge of these Spirituals, such as setting them down in

Carl Van Vechten/The Van Vechten Trust

American composer and singer Harry T. Burleigh (1866-1949)

print[2], and taking the songs to a larger audience through means of concerts, as was done by the famous Fisk Jubilee Singers, and soon by other ensembles.

In this context, in 1892, Harry Burleigh arrived in Manhattan from his hometown of Erie, Pennsylvania, where his parents had came to live from the South, where they had been born into slavery. Burleigh, an obvious young talent, was the recipient of a scholarship from the National Conservatory of Music, newly founded in New York City. The mission of this effort was to train musicians in principles of Classical composition and performance for the ongoing cultural advancement of the nation. The effort emphatically included making use of heritage folk music, as well as entirely new compositions—as demonstrated by the masters Mozart, Beethoven, Brahms and others. Johannes Brahms personally encouraged the National Conservatory of Music, and backed Antonín Dvořák to go to New York City in 1892, to teach music at the new center. Philanthropist Jeannette M. Thurber was the principal funder of the Conservatory.

Burleigh and Dvořák

A wonderful, productive collaboration ensued between Burleigh and Dvořák. It is reported that Burleigh,

---

1. *Burleigh and the Battle for American Classical Music*, book review, *EIR* (Vol. 21, No. 22, May 27, 1994), by Susan Bowen.

2. See R. Nathaniel Dett, *Religious Folk-Songs Of The Negro: As Sung At Hampton Institute*, for an early collection of songs. (Hampton, Va.: Hampton Institute Press, 1927).

an extraordinarily fine baritone, spent many days singing to Dvořák—at Dvořák's request, the Negro songs he knew as plantation melodies, and other tunes; for example, those said to be sung along the Underground Railway stops, which he remembered hearing as a child. Burleigh later reflected, after his last public concert in 1944, that, "Under the inspiration of Dvořák, I became convinced that the Spirituals were not meant for the colored people, but for all people."

Burleigh went on to create beautiful settings for Spirituals as well as to compose other vocal works, and, in effect, campaign for creativity. In New York City, he created the "lecture-recital"—a concert where his singing of the Spirituals was preceded by a presentation on each song's background and significance, in order to elevate the audience's understanding of what he considered to be sacred works. He sang for decades as cantor at Manhattan's Temple Emanu-El, and St. George's Episcopal Church, which originally came about only after Burleigh had to break the color taboo. For years, he taught and worked in Italy, as well as in Manhattan, and his music was published by Milan-based Ricordi, Verdi's publisher. He was directly involved in internationally promoting the Italian Bel Canto school.

Dvořák went on to produce works in America that are among his most famous, reflecting the universal treasure of the Spirituals. The theme known as "Goin' Home" (words were later put to his melody by one of his students), is a Dvořák original, often mis-thought to be a heritage Spiritual. It is featured also in his New World Symphony. Less known are the cultural bombshells he set off in New York City. In 1892 Dvořák held a fundraiser concert, dedicated to Harry Burleigh, with an all African-American chorus, and integrated orchestra, doing choral pieces, including his own adaptation of "Old Folks at Home" from Stephen Foster. Dvořák wrote a guest article in 1895, titled "Music in America" (in Harper's *The New Monthly Magazine*), in which he reiterated his view that, for the United States, "inspiration for truly national music might be derived from the

Composer and conductor Hall Johnson (1888-1970)

Negro melodies or Indian chants. I was led to take this view partly by the fact that the so-called plantation songs are indeed the most striking and appealing melodies that have yet been found on this side of the water..."[3]

The impetus for advancing Classical culture was seen in follow-on initiatives, most prominently in New York City, and in certain other locations. Burleigh's urging of a "re-birth" for the Spirituals led to the start of what later became known as the "Harlem Renaissance" Movement in Manhattan. Burleigh was in discussions with poets, including Paul Laurence Dunbar, and composers Samuel Coleridge-Taylor, and James Weldon Johnson, one of the founders of the National Association of Negro Musicians (1919). Johnson and his brother Rosamund Johnson, prepared settings of Spirituals. The singer, composer Roland Hayes did major work.

Hall Johnson

In the midst of this, Hall Johnson (1888-1970), African-American composer and conductor, came on the scene in New York. He said at one point, "I felt that the work and folk songs of my people and their spirituals offered a rich and untapped field. I wanted to give that music to the world." Originally from South Carolina, he was highly trained musically at a sequence of institutions: first, the Allen University at Columbia, S.C.; then on to the University of Pennsylvania in 1910; he next studied composition at the Juilliard School of Music in Manhattan. He settled in New York City in 1914.

In September 1925, he established the Hall Johnson Choir, which continued for the next 30 years in New York, performing in top venues, and gaining international acclaim. In 1946, Johnson additionally formed the Festival Negro Chorus of New York City, which, he said, was to "strengthen racial unity and to promote

3. "Music in America" by Antonín Dvořák, in Harper's *New Monthly Magazine,* Vol. XC, February 1895, pp. 429-434. Reprinted in *EIR,* Vol. 20, No. 32, August 20, 1993, *Antonín Dvořák: Creating a Truly American Music,* by Kathy Wolfe and Marcia Merry.

Members of the internationally acclaimed, Harlem-based Hall Johnson Choir singing in the film "The Green Pastures."

racial harmony." In 1951, Johnson and his chorus performed in Berlin at the International Festival of Fine Arts, officially representing the United States. The audiences, and even critics, were entranced.

By most accounts, Hall Johnson arranged nearly 500 songs for his choir members. He did research, taught and wrote, and coached his singers to perfection. Among the many great singers and musicians associated with Johnson's work and mission were Marian Anderson and more recently, Schiller Institute collaborators Sylvia Olden Lee and Robert McFerrin, and Schiller Institute Board Member William Warfield.

Under Assault

To complete this short account of New York City and the Spiritual, there must be added the terrible side of the history: the assault against the Negro Spiritual and Classical culture of any kind in the United States. This emanated directly from London, the seat of British imperial power, and took many forms, from racism, financial warfare, and threats, to inducement to corruption.

To begin with, the National Conservatory of Music itself was thwarted. It operated throughout its existence under pressure of all kinds. Instead, New York City became home to several points of subversion of music. Tin Pan Alley came into being, to promote the most banal, repetitive, and also racist sounds, called "popular" music. In the 1920s, this was furthered, with the advent of "entertainment radio."

In 1937, the NBC Symphony Orchestra was founded as a radio orchestra, which brought in Arturo Toscanini, the infamous conductor who played "by the notes," and not by the music. All across the country, there were pressures to close down local choral societies and opera houses, German-inspired *Lieder* circles, and local bands and orchestras. Church networks were induced to forego parts-singing and polyphony, in favor of single melody lines, and gospel.

An operation to banalize and corrupt the Spirituals was waged, offering opportunities on Broadway and in Hollywood, for "Negro" music, especially ragtime and jazz.

In 1922, Harry Burleigh wrote a letter to the National Association for the Advancement of Colored People, denouncing this kind of degradation as a "growing tendency of some of our musicians to utilize the melodies of our Spirituals in fox-trots, dance numbers and semi-sentimental songs...."

Instead, referring to Spirituals as "prayer-songs," he said, "These melodies are our prized possession... In them, we have a mine of... local wealth that is everlasting. Into their making was poured the aspiration of a race in bondage, whose religion—intensely felt—was their whole hope and comfort, and the only vehicle through which their inner spirits soared free.

"They rank with the great folk-music of the world and are among the loveliest of chanted prayers...."[4]

Harry Burleigh's impassioned call to beauty and meaning, speaks to us yet again today, as the intent of the Manhattan Project to re-establish the choral principle in the United States for the benefit of all mankind.

Further Reading:
- "The African-American Spiritual and the Resurrection of Classical Art: Not Force, But Beauty, Will Change America," by Dennis Speed, Oct. 9, 1995, Schiller Institute.
- "The 'New Negro' Choral Legacy of Hall Johnson," by Marva Griffin Carter, in *Chorus and Community,* ed. Karen Ahlquist (Chicago: University of Illinois Press), 2006.

_____

4. Harry T. Burleigh to the NAACP, Nov. 10, 1922. (Found in Dennis Speed article; cited in *Further Reading*, above.)

Every Day Counts In Today's Showdown To Save Civilization

That's why you need EIR's **Daily Alert Service**, a strategic overview compiled with the input of Lyndon LaRouche, and delivered to your email 5 days a week.

For example: On November 5, EIR's Daily Alert featured Lyndon LaRouche's warning that Obama can and must be removed immediately, to avoid Obama's push for thermonuclear confrontation with Russia. That issue identified The Drone Papers put out by Glenn Greenwald's The Intercept as the Pentagon Papers of 2015—damning Barack Obama as a mass murderer, and providing the evidence for his Constitutional removal from office.

That edition also featured EIR's exclusive report on a hearing called by Rep. John Conyers on Capitol Hill to expose the dangers represented by Obama's actions—a hearing all but suppressed by other media.

This is intelligence you need to act on, if we are going to survive as a nation and a species. Can you really afford to be without it?

THURSDAY, NOVEMBER 5, 2015

EIR Daily Alert Service

EIR DAILY ALERT SERVICE P.O. BOX 17390, WASHINGTON, DC 20041-0390

- Dump Obama Now or Face Thermonuclear Holocaust
- Extraordinary Capitol Hill Event Warns of Obama Thermonuclear War Provocations against Russia
- Rep. Tulsi Gabbard: Unlawful for U.S. To Wage War in Syria
- Satanic Environmentalist Offensive Launched in U.S.
- O'Malley Campaign Support Grows in Iowa, Key Democrats Say
- Behind the New York Times Headlines on 'Death in Middle Age'
- QE Inflated Wall Street, Screwed Main Street—Says Wall Street
- Russian Defense Ministry Coordinating with Syrian Opposition against ISIS
- Frontex: Arrest Illegal Immigrants!
- Bavaria Considering a Constitutional Case against Merkel
- U.S.-Russian Communications Test over Syria
- Malaysia and ASEAN Stand Up To Obama's Threats over South China Sea
- Barenboim's Orchestra Plays Mozart for Peace in the Middle East

EDITORIAL

Dump Obama Now or Face Thermonuclear Holocaust

✂

LaRouches Address Conference in Russia

Dec. 22—The 5th International Conference on Fundamental and Applied Problems of Sustained Development in the System "Nature—Society—Man" opened yesterday at Dubna State University in the Moscow Region, near Russia's capital.

This year's conference title is "Problems of Measuring and Managing Sustained Development in the Face of Global Challenges, Risks and Threats," with a special focus on the significance and potential of China's Silk Road Economic Belt for all Eurasia.

Greetings to the conference from American economist Lyndon LaRouche and a video-taped speech by Schiller Institute founder Helga Zepp-LaRouche were highlights of the opening plenary session.

The Dubna conferences were initiated in 2010 by Prof. Boris Bolshakov, a close associate of the late Pobisk Kuznetsov, a Russian visionary scientist and organizer of industry, who in the last years of his life became a friend and dialogue partner of LaRouche. Officially held by the P.G. Kuznetsov International School of Sustained Development, the conference was hosted by Dubna State University and co-sponsored by the Russian Academy of Sciences, the Russian Academy of Natural Sciences, the Russian Academy of Engineering, and the Kazakhstan National Academy of Natural Sciences. Upwards of 200 people took part over the two days, with attendance from several regions of Russia, as well as Belarus and Kazakhstan.

LaRouche's greetings (below) emphasized "the special task and responsibility of science to provide the human race with a perspective for a sustainable existence as a galactic species," citing the exemplary work of Academician Vladimir Vernadsky. This was one of two messages presented during the opening of the conference, the other being from Ms. Na Jinhua, president of the Jiangxi Science and Technology Normal University, China.

During the plenary session, Helga Zepp-LaRouche's video on the Silk Road electrified the audience. Recorded November 10 for conferences in Colombia and Mexico, as well as the Dubna conference, it was presented in Dubna under the title "The Strategic Significance of the New Silk Road." (It is posted online; the title pages and subtitles are in Russian, with the audio in English.) When the video ended, most of the audience burst into applause.

Greetings from Lyndon LaRouche

Dec. 21—This message from Lyndon LaRouche was presented today to the conference at Dubna, Russia.

The world has never been in such a peril as it is at the present time, when the combination of the pending disintegration of the trans-Atlantic financial system and the related danger of a geopolitically motivated thermonuclear extinction is putting the future of mankind into jeopardy.

In these times it is the special task and responsibility of science to provide the human race with a perspective for a sustainable existence as a galactic species, as the only species known in the universe so far, whose creativity can again and again break through the boundaries of existing knowledge, reaching deeper and deeper into the inner lawfulness of the physical universe, of which human creativity is the most advanced expression.

If this world is to be saved—and it must and it will—it is the living tradition of such great minds as Vladimir Vernadsky and Pobisk Kuznetsov, which will show the pathway. We must encourage young scientists from the entire world, to come forward with new creative ideas to define the next epoch of civilization, an epoch of creativity per se, as the only condition, worthy of the dignity of man. I wish your conference all possible success and remain yours,

Lyndon LaRouche
18 December 2015

The Promise and the Vision Of the New Silk Road

The following presentation was recorded by Helga Zepp-LaRouche on Nov. 10, 2015, for a series of conferences which she could not attend personally, including the one in Dubna Dec. 21. Zepp-LaRouche is the founder of the Schiller Institutes and chairwoman of the German political party Civil Rights Movement Solidarity.

Hello! I send greetings to your conference. I want to talk to you about the vision which is embedded in the New Silk Road,—which is the policy initiated by Chinese President Xi Jinping in 2013 and which is quickly unfolding to become the most promising dynamic on the planet.

But let me briefly tell you why it is so extremely important that people start to look at this new model of economics. The underlying dynamic behind all major crises in the world, from the wars in various parts of the world, to terrorism, to many other social crises, is that the trans-Atlantic financial system is about to blow out in ways which will make 2008 look like the proverbial peanuts, if it comes to that, and if it is not prevented ahead of time.

Now you also have an unbelievable economic and social collapse in the United States. According to a report just published in the *New York Times,* the death rate of white Americans in the middle-age bracket of 45-54 years of age, has increased by 10% on average, and for the poor it has increased by 22%. Now, that's not supposed to happen. People are not supposed to die when they are in the middle of their lives. And the only comparison to such an event, was what happened in Russia after the collapse of the Soviet Union in the '90s

Schiller Institute

Helga Zepp-LaRouche presenting the New Silk Road alternative to the current world crisis, in a video done for a series of conferences, including the one in Dubna, Russia.

during the Yeltsin period, at which point basically one million people disappeared from the demographic statistics every year. This decline ended only after President Putin came to power.

Now, what is causing these deaths among these middle-aged Americans? It's drug addiction, deaths by drugs, alcohol, and suicides. And that is obviously a reflection of the fact that the general mood in America has shifted from the optimism of the Kennedy period, to the present time, in which most Americans are pessimistic about the future. They believe that coming generations will be much worse off than the present one. This is the first time in the so-called advanced world, in which such an idea could be accepted. It used to be the basis of morality, that parents would say, "I want my children to be better off than myself."

Now, that has vanished. And if you look at it, you have people in many areas who have lost income; the living standard is collapsing. People have to work two or three jobs. Take drug addiction in Baltimore, for example: One out of every ten people is a heroin user. There's a heroin epidemic! A lot of the heroin is coming from Latin America. The United States is being flooded, and many people become addicted, because heroin now costs 25% of the price of prescription drugs. So the whole country is really collapsing.

And in Europe, it is no better. It is different, but not better. You probably have heard reports of an unprecedented refugee crisis, which comes mostly from Southwest Asia, from these wars which are based on lies. Now you have refugees from Iraq, Syria, Afghanistan, and Yemen, but also from many countries in Africa. There are presently 60 million people already in various states of being refugees and many of them have the desire to go to Europe; that is destabilizing the very foundations of Europe at this point.

Now, I could mention more of such horrible developments, but the overall picture makes it very clear: We must have a paradigm shift. We must go to a completely different economic model. And that is why the New Silk Road is so extremely important.

The New Silk Road in Action

In 2013 in Kazakhstan, President Xi Jinping announced the New Silk Road policy. In November, he announced the Maritime Silk Road policy. Then the BRICS countries practically joined the New Silk Road movement, which was first demonstrated at the BRICS heads of state summit in Fortaleza, Brazil, in 2014. This thrust was consolidated at the Ufa BRICS summit this year in Russia.

What is unfolding is a completely new dynamic, based on totally different principles than the casino economy of the trans-Atlantic sector. Remember that the ancient Silk Road was an exchange not only of goods such as porcelains and silk, but also of technologies: How to make porcelain, how to make silk—an exchange of culture and ideas. And that is exactly what has been revived right now by President Xi Jinping, who has explicitly said that every country that participates in this Silk Road development, will benefit from a "win-win" perspective: that it is in the interest of every country participating in it.

Now with an unbelievably rapid pace, new trade routes have developed in the last year: from Chengdu in China, Yiwu, Chongqing, Xi'an, and Lianyungang. Now, every week trains are leaving full of goods for such places in Europe as Duisburg and Hamburg in Germany, Madrid in Spain, or Lyon in France.

Now, this development fever, one can say, has already caught on in Central Asia and the Balkans. Countries in the Balkans are looking to China for infrastructure development, and not the EU. But the vision of the Silk Road has also caught on in Europe. A couple of weeks ago, Xi Jinping was in Great Britain, and the British, being always very smart to be first to smell the new breezes, not only made massive trade arrangements and trade deals with China, but they said that the "Golden Age" of British-Chinese relations is about to begin.

In addition, German Chancellor Angela Merkel has just been in China, and she concluded many, many trade deals. But even more important, they combined the complementary aspects of their economies to form an economic powerhouse. China just did the same thing, by the way, with South Korea and Japan; this is obviously very, very important for overcoming the conflicts in the South China Sea.

But that is not all. In Spain there was just a very important forum on the Silk Road, where the leader of the most important development agency of China used the beautiful image that the Silk Road can and must become a "Noah's Ark" for all the countries in trouble around the world.

That is especially important for Southwest Asia and Africa, the sources of the big, big refugee crisis which is destabilizing all of Europe right now. It is obvious that if one takes the Silk Road, which now goes from China through Central Asia, all the way to Europe, and then extend that into Southwest Asia—to build infrastructure, integrated systems of fast trains, waterways, of highways, of declaring war against the deserts by tapping into new fresh water sources through large amounts of desalination of ocean water using nuclear energy, and by ionizing the moisture in the atmosphere to create rainfall, thus creating new rain and weather patterns to declare war on the deserts—in this way, one creates the precondition for new cities, for industry, for agriculture in those regions too.

I don't want to use the word "Marshall Plan," because it's a slightly different conception, but it is a kind of a Marshall Plan, because that gives you the idea that it *is* possible through directed state intervention and economic policy based on physical principles to overcome any economic crisis, as the Marshall Plan did for Europe.

If all the great neighbors of the Middle East and Near East—Russia, China, India, Iran, Egypt, and the European countries, which are now destabilized by refugees—were to say: Let's together make a Marshall Plan for the Middle East and invite the United States to be part of it, I think that there is an absolute reason to believe that the problem of terrorism could be overcome. With such a vision of hope, you could persuade many young people, especially young men, not to join the jihad, but to fight for a better future, to become scientists, to become engineers, and to create a family, and to have a future.

Obviously the same is true for Africa, where now millions of people are fleeing, taking the 50% risk of not making it by getting into little boats in the Mediterranean, where about 6,000 or more officially have drowned already *this year;* and people still take that risk to get to Europe.

Now if we were to do the same thing with Africa, and say, "Let's extend the Silk Road together, let's join all the countries and develop Africa," I think we could eliminate poverty and create stability in a very, very short period of time.

The Common Aims of Mankind

Now, why am I so optimistic? Well, if you look at the China model of economy, China has created an economic miracle, which apart from the German economic miracle in the postwar period is really without any precedent. China has replicated in only 30 years, what America and Europe needed 200 years to accomplish. And with that economic method, they have eliminated poverty, they have elevated 600 million people out of poverty; and the intention is to use the Silk Road development to basically make the same thing possible for people in the interior regions in western China.

Why is this functioning? And what can we learn from this Chinese model?

I have been to China many times, and I am convinced that this rapid economic growth is based on the Confucian tradition of China, which put a very high premium on excellence in education. Confucius said, rejuvenate yourself every day, develop a new idea every day; never the same thing twice, always improve yourself; perfect yourself every day. And that is the principle which China has applied and is applying especially to the education of the young, the students, pupils, also women. It has put a very big emphasis on achieving gender equality by having as many women as men participate in university education. This year they are graduating 2,000 students in the area of fusion power [engineering] alone, and I don't know of any country in Europe or the Americas which comes close to such a rate of progress.

But China has not only created a "win-win perspective" with the Silk Road for other countries to join. It has also put up a new model of foreign relations, which is based on the idea of respect for sovereignty, respect for the difference of the social model of the other country, and non-interference. It has invited the United States and the Americas to join. And here, you see behind me the world map of projects from *EIR*'s special report, "The New Silk Road Becomes the World Land-Bridge." It is a model of how to transform the underdevelopment of every part of the world, and create instead a completely new paradigm.

What is this New Silk Road, World Land-Bridge policy? It is an effort to overcome geopolitics—geopolitics, which was the cause for two world wars in the Twentieth Century—which is the idea that a group of nations or one nation has a legitimate interest which it must defend against other nations, if need be, by military means. That kind of thinking has to be eliminated, because in an age of thermonuclear weapons, war cannot be a means of conflict resolution any more.

So, we have to replace the idea of geopolitics with the idea of the common aims of mankind. And there are many common aims of mankind! For example the elimination of poverty, which would be very easy. We could get rid of poverty in a year, in two years,—very easy. We have to protect our planet, which after all is only a tiny blue planet, in the big Solar System, in an even bigger Galaxy, and our Galaxy is only one of billions of galaxies. So our very little blue planet is really very precious to us, and it must be protected against asteroids, comets, and other dangers from outer space.

To do that, we should explore space. We should travel through space. We should develop technologies which allow us to do that. And China, again, presently has the most advanced space program in the world. With its lunar missions, it is preparing to mine helium-3 from the Moon, and bring it back in a couple of years in large quantities, because it does not exist in that form in big quantities on Earth, and use it as a fuel for the future fusion economy on Earth.

Presently there are many reports indicating that fusion breakthroughs are very close. If we reach fusion, we can have raw materials security and energy security for a very long time—for tens of thousands of years. Helium-3 will already be the second generation of fusion economy, basically changing all the physical principles we rely on, and also allowing us to use fusion power for space travel.

So, there are many good things in the future. But I think we have to really fight for this model. I think it is within mankind's reach, that every child on the planet could have access to universal education. And if that

happens, oligarchism will disappear. Moreover, if every child can have access to all areas of knowledge in order to develop the fullest potential which is embedded in each human person, more and more people will become truly human, more and more individuals will become geniuses, and we are only at the embryonic age of mankind.

Just think, in the last ten thousand years—that's not a long time, if you compare it with the age of the universe, or even of our planet—how much development did man accomplish? From a population potential of maybe a couple of million people who were hunters and gatherers, we now have 7 billion people. And we have unbelievable technologies, you know, we can communicate, we can do all kinds of things. But for the next ten thousand years, we can explore the riches of our universe, which we presently do not even know exist.

But we must have that kind of optimism, that we are on the verge of humanity becoming the truly creative species. And I think that is the promise and the vision of the Silk Road. So, join it and study it.

Flashback: How MI6, the CIA and The Saudis Launched Jihad

by Jeffrey Steinberg

Visas for Al Qaeda—the CIA Handouts That Rocked the World
by J. Michael Springmann
Washington, D.C.: Daena Publishers LLC, 2015
283 pages, paperback, $17.50, Kindle, $10.00.

Dec. 29—J. Michael Springmann has a sordid tale to tell. As an entry-level American diplomat in the late 1980s, his first overseas assignment was in Jeddah, Saudi Arabia, where he was a consular officer responsible for approving visas for non-immigrant visitors to the United States. In the course of his two-year assignment in Jeddah, he witnessed the flow of terrorists from all over the world into the United States, under a CIA program that he dubbed "Visas for Terrorists."

When Springmann attempted to do his job—which was to screen applicants and reject those who did not meet the strict criteria spelled out in State Department guidelines and Federal laws—he found himself up against a majority of his colleagues in Jeddah, at the embassy in Riyadh, and back home at Foggy Bottom and CIA headquarters in Langley. His decisions to block visa applications for a small army of suspect characters with no apparent reason for traveling to the United States, and with no ties to Saudi Arabia or to their home countries, were routinely reversed by higher-ups in Jeddah.

He spent 1987-1989 in Jeddah, and was later assigned to Stuttgart, Germany, New Delhi, India, and

Springmann's personal account, published in 2014.

eventually to a cubby-hole desk at the State Department's in-house intelligence agency, the Bureau of Intelligence and Research (INR). In 1991, with no explanation, he was terminated. He later found out that his supervisor in Jeddah, Jay Freres, had filled his personnel file with scurrilous, but vaguely worded complaints, which he never was able to see, even after he was dumped in late 1991 and spent the next decade battling through appeals, Freedom of Information Act suits, and efforts to alert Congressional oversight committees and major media outlets.

His personal account offers a small window into a very big national security scandal. In effect, successive U.S. administrations, beginning in 1979, recruited, trained, and deployed thousands of what Springmann called the Arab-Afghan Legion. When the Soviet Union pulled out of Afghanistan, after more than a decade of warfare against the Arab-Afghan Legion, the program continued, unabated. When the Soviet Union and the Warsaw Pact collapsed, the program continued, unabated. The same terrorists who had been deployed against the Red Army were the shock-troops for British-American-Saudi regime-change projects, starting in the Balkans, and moving on to Iraq, Libya, and Syria.

Jeddah

During the more than two years that Springmann served in Jeddah, the consulate issued 45,000 visas per year. He personally processed 100 visa applications per day. Soon after his arrival in Jeddah, Springmann discovered that, of the 20 diplomatic personnel assigned to the Consulate, he and two others were the only legitimate Foreign Service Officers. The rest were either CIA or National Security Agency personnel, operating under State Department cover. For the most part, they were recruiters and facilitators of the flow of terrorists, criminals, and would-be jihadists through various circuitous routes into Afghanistan and Pakistan.

Springmann's first career-ending mistake took place during a visit of Joseph P. O'Neill, who led an inspection team from the State Department's watchdog Inspection Corps. Under questioning from O'Neill, Springmann revealed that he had rejected visa applications made by scores of suspect individuals, only to have his decisions reversed and the questionable visas issued. Springmann told O'Neill that he had retained a file of all of the rejected visa applications, with background data on why he had rejected the applications. Mysteriously, soon after his meeting with O'Neill, Springmann's list was shredded, and all records of the Arab-Afghan visa cases disappeared.

Through contacts with other State Department personnel, DIA officers, and others, Springmann learned that there were three "recruiting stations" in Saudi Arabia for funnelling fighters through the United States and other destinations into Afghanistan. The stations were located in Jeddah, Riyadh, and in the al-Sharqiyah Province. He later discovered that there were as many as 52 similar recruiting stations peppered throughout the United States, with the largest in Brooklyn, New York. Phoenix, Boston, Chicago, Tucson, Minnesota, Washington, D.C., and Washington State were all recruiting centers, targeting Muslim communities and African-American neighborhoods.

Springmann not only earned the hatred of the Arab-Afghan Legion recruiters and facilitators in Jeddah for questioning the flow of unsavory characters into the United States through the Jeddah consulate. Through his communications with foreign embassy intelligence personnel, he stumbled upon the fact that Saudi Arabia was secretly importing Intermediate Range Ballistic Missiles (IRBMs) from China. The CIA and NSA stations in Riyadh and Jeddah had completely missed the transaction, which had been secretly arranged by Saudi Arabia's ambassador in Washington, Prince Bandar bin-Sultan. (Prince Bandar would figure prominently in the Joint Congressional Inquiry into 9/11, having provided at least $50-72,000 to two of

Author J. Michael Springmann, consular officer in Jeddah, Saudi Arabia, 1987-1989.

the lead hijackers, according to the 28-page chapter from the Joint Inquiry report which has been suppressed by Presidents George W. Bush and Barack Obama.)

Apparently the American spooks operating out of the Kingdom were preoccupied with the Afghan project and had abandoned all other intelligence responsibilities.

Springmann later learned that his intelligence missives from Jeddah made it into the President's Daily Briefing on more than one occasion.

The Strange Case of Ali Mohamed

Springmann's experiences in Jeddah overlapped the activities of one Ali Abdul Saoud Mohamed, a major in Egyptian Military Intelligence, who worked for the CIA on the Arab-Afghan Legions program. To this day, Mohamed's activities are shrouded in mystery and official secrets.

Major Mohamed was supposedly kicked out of the Egyptian Army in the mid-1980s, based on evidence that he was a secret member of the Egyptian Islamic Jihad organization, a terrorist group that was responsible for the 1981 assassination of Egyptian President Anwar Sadat. U.S. sources report that Major Mohamed was actually a double-agent, working for both Egyptian Military Intelligence and the CIA, penetrating the terrorist group.

In 1984, Ali Mohamed had walked into the U.S. Embassy in Cairo and offered his services to the CIA. In the subsequent years, he served as a liaison to various terrorist cells that were recruited to fight against the Soviets in Afghanistan. At one point, Major Mo-

Ali Abdul Saoud Mohamed. As a sergeant in the U.S. Army, he is reported to have trained Osama bin Laden and Ayman al-Zawahiri.

hamed accompanied Ayman al-Zawahiri, the head of the Egyptian Islamic Jihad, and currently the head of al-Qaeda, on a fundraising tour of the United States, soliciting private funds for the Afghan mujahideen cause.

Major Mohamed would marry an American woman and join the U.S. Army Special Forces. He spent several years teaching unconventional warfare and Arabic courses at the JFK Special Warfare School at Fort Bragg, N.C. While serving in the U.S. Army and with the CIA, Mohamed made 57 trips to Afghanistan.

During his visits to South Asia, now Sgt. Mohamed, U.S. Army, wrote the terrorist training manual and playbook for al-Qaeda. He personally trained al-Zawahiri and Osama bin-Laden, along with countless other Arab-Afghan Legion fighters. Several of Sgt. Mohamed's "recruits" carried out the 1993 World Trade Center bombing. One of his American "students," El Sayyid Nosair, was convicted of plotting to bomb United Nations headquarters in New York.

In the mid-1990s, Sgt. Mohamed traveled to Africa, where he set up a number of al-Qaeda front companies to generate the funds for the 1998 bombings of the U.S. embassies in Kenya and Tanzania. He did the on-the-ground site profiling prior to the al-Qaeda bombings.

Within the al-Qaeda orbit, Sgt. Mohamed was known as Abu Mohamed al-Amriki ("the American").

On the surface, it appeared that justice finally caught up with Sgt. Mohamed. Following the African embassy bombings, Mohamed's California apartment was raided by the FBI. Computer drives and documents proved his involvement in the planning of the attacks, which were the most deadly actions to date by al-Qaeda. Sgt. Mohamed was subpoenaed to testify before a Federal grand jury, and he was subsequently indicted.

In September 2000, Ali Mohamed reached a plea agreement, admitting to his role in the Africa embassy scheme. As of 2011, however, according to former FBI Special Agent Ali Soufan, he had not yet been sentenced.

A source familiar with the case reported to this author that there were "problems" with the evidence against Sgt. Mohamed. It seemed that prosecutors could not prove that his activities were not sanctioned either by Egyptian intelligence or the CIA. The deal that he struck included a guarantee that he would never be sentenced or serve any time in jail. In return, he provided a treasure trove of inside information on the first generation of al-Qaeda.

The Deeper Truth

These simple explanations hide a much deeper and murkier truth. The United States, Great Britain, and Saudi Arabia colluded to drive the Soviet Red Army out of Afghanistan, using an international unconventional army made up of avowed jihadists, criminals, and mercenaries. That Foreign Legion continued to operate, grow, and morph into al-Qaeda, the Islamic State, and scores of other jihadist groups.

It would also appear that the Visas for Terrorists program grew and prospered, with disastrous consequences. Between 2000 and 2001, 15 of the 19 September 11, 2001 terrorists got their visas to enter the United States from the Consulate in Jeddah.

While these revelations are not new—the Springmann book first appeared, with virtually no media coverage, in 2014, and the Ali Mohamed case briefly grabbed news attention following the 9/11 attacks—they offer yet another powerful argument for the immediate declassification of the 28-page chapter from the original Joint Congressional Inquiry into 9/11—a chapter that highlights the Saudi funding of the terrorists.

It also makes clear that the real story of 9/11 is much nastier than just the Saudi role, and puts the issue of the British role and the involvement of contaminated elements of the U.S. intelligence establishment under a new spotlight.

What Economic Path for China?

by William Jones

The Myth of Free Trade: An Inquiry into British and American Industrialization
by Mei Junjie
Beijing: Xinhua Publishing House, 2014
342 pages, hardback, in Chinese, second edition,
¥35.50.

Dec. 20—Dr. Mei Junjie, the author of *The Myth of Free Trade,* is a senior fellow of international political economy at the Shanghai Academy of Social Sciences (SASS), and since 2000 has served as director of the SASS Center for World Economic History. He is also the founding executive director of the SASS Institute of China Studies. He received his Ph.D. in international economics from SASS, an M.S. in the politics of the world economy from the London School of Economics, and an M.A. in world modernization studies from Peking University.

Mei was a Chevening Scholar of the British Foreign and Commonwealth Office and a visiting researcher at Stanford University. He has taught international trade policy at Shanghai Maritime University, conducted policy analysis at the Pudong Institute of Development Studies, and taught language students at Nanjing University.

Dr. Mei has published extensively on issues of international political economy, his best-known work being the one abstracted here, *The Myth of Free Trade: an Inquiry into British and American Industrialization* (Xinhua Publishing House, 2014; Shanghai Sanlian Press, 2008). He is co-editor-in-chief of the book series

Author Mei Junjie, senior fellow of international political economy at the Shanghai Academy of Social Sciences

on "World Economic History" published by the prestigious Commercial Press in China, and is also the editor-in-chief of the book series on "Global Economic Strategists" issued by the Shanghai Far East Publishing House.

Mei has translated numerous works into Chinese such as *Industry and Empire* (Eric Hobsbawm, 1999), *Against the Tide: An Intellectual History of Free Trade* (Douglas Irwin, 1996), *Count Sergei Witte and the Twilight of Imperial Russia* (Sidney Harcave, 2004), and *Jean-Baptiste Colbert* (Ines Murat, 1980). He is now engaged in a project to translate some of the works by and about Friedrich List, the German-American economist who had some influence on Chinese economic policy in the last century, as he did in many other countries.

China Seeks Its Own Path to Development

China currently finds itself in a stage of dramatic transformation. The world has been astonished by the rapid economic development of China over the last 30 years, since the initiation by Deng Xiaoping's "reform and opening up" policy. China re-entered the world economy, so to speak, as a cheap-labor producer for the world market, but has in the process transformed itself into something much more important. Meanwhile the financial collapse of the world economy has destroyed the export market for which China produced. China thus finds itself in a situation where it must carve out a new path, or as they call it "a new normal." This has occasioned a major debate in China over the economic policy it must adopt.

While tremendous pressure has been placed on China by forces in the West to simply open its markets to "free trade," as implemented with such devastating results by Russia in the 1990s, Chinese policy makers have been very reluctant to travel that route. Nevertheless, there is a significant faction of Chinese economists who are pushing in that direction, foolishly believing that eliminating all government "interference" will suddenly unleash a wave of innovation and creativity. The late Milton Friedman, that gadfly of "free trade unlimited," has his followers in the People's Republic of China.

And yet, while there are still those who long for the days of the old "command economy" before "reform and opening up," it is clear that those days (which can be viewed as "prosperous" only under a very thick film of nostalgia), are definitely not coming back. While the nation will continue to rely on state direction of the economy, there will be a transition away from the traditional state-owned enterprises, which still remain a mainstay of the Chinese economy, toward the creation of a *Mittelstand,* namely, small and medium-sized companies which have always proven to be the mainstay of innovation.

New Interest in the 'American System'

In seeking a "China path" toward reaching the goal of a moderately well-off society by the middle of this century, there has been renewed interest in the "American System" and its economists, such as Alexander Hamilton and Friedrich List, and its more recent representative, economist and statesman Lyndon LaRouche. A number of economists, such as Professor Mei Junjie, are looking at the work of these exponents of the American System to extract from them lessons for China today.

Other leading economists, such as Professor Ding Yifan, have relied on LaRouche's notion of "physical economy" to develop his own concept of a "knowledge-based economy," which is now generally regarded as a key element in China's new economic strategy. The work of List is particularly relevant now, because of the crucial role his work played in the Bismarck reforms; China looks upon Germany, and its hitherto successful development of a *Mittelstand,* as a model for what it would like to develop.

List's understanding may well have also played a role in China's "One Belt, One Road" policy, given

German-American economist Friedrich List

that List has been more of a guiding figure for Chinese economists than even Adam Smith. For List, more than anyone, understood the strategic and economic significance of the railroad as a stimulus to economic development.

The development policy now being pursued by the Chinese government would surely bring a smile to the lips of this German economist, who spent most of his life teaching European leaders the importance of the railroad as a transmission belt for science and technology. List also envisioned the development of a continental railroad "landbridge" that would bring together the nations of the Eurasian continent—as has been developed by China. Many of List's insights in this regard could still be very stimulating for Chinese planners as the Silk Road Economic Belt moves forward.

We look forward to the work that Professor Mei is now pursuing in translating into Chinese some of the works of and about Friedrich List. We are confident that this body of knowledge will help inform Chinese policy makers in formulating their own blueprint for development, as all the other models put forward have already proven themselves to be such dismal failures.

Free trade in action: British ships bombard Hong Kong harbor during the First Opium War.

The following abstract of the *The Myth of Free Trade,* kindly provided by Professor Mei, has been edited.

William Jones may be contacted at cuth@erols.com

Abstract: The Myth of Free Trade

by Mei Junjie

It is generally believed that removing trade barriers will increase the welfare of the trading parties concerned and that trade liberalization, or even free trade, is a sure way for developing countries to reduce poverty and achieve economic prosperity. Indeed, the policy recipe known as the "Washington consensus" has invariably included recommendations to open markets and deregulate. Underlying this economic school of thought is a widely accepted belief that it was Adam Smith, the acknowledged protagonist of liberalism, who laid the foundation of the British industrial revolution and, more broadly, that the modern rise of the western world has been due to free trade and laissez-faire. Such a liberal mindset has also found its way into the academic and policy-making circles in China.

However, nothing could be further from the truth. The liberal economic thinking, including its interpretation of history, is erroneous and misleading. This book empirically surveys the history of British and American industrial development over several centuries and reveals the falsity of the liberal claims. Evidence shows that, contrary to the tenets of the free trade doctrine, both Britain and America engaged in long-term and highly protectionist trade practices during their industrialization. It was only after trade protection had afforded them predominant industrial superiority that they turned to free trade. The main findings of the book are as follows:

The prevailing notion that liberal economic theories and practices enabled Britain to attain its industrial supremacy is not supported by the facts. Free trade did not motivate the British industrial revolution. Instead, it was Britain's industrial supremacy, nurtured by protectionism, that canonized the free trade doctrine. Adam Smith and his doctrine, while displaying little intellectual originality, came to be revered decades after his death chiefly because the British needed new leverage for pursuing their national interests. By creating such an ideology, free traders hoped to cajole the less-developed countries into an asymmetrical economic relationship with the more developed Britain.

The woolen goods production grew into the staple industry in Britain thanks to the persistent restrictions placed on the free export of British wool and the free import of foreign woolen products. Likewise, the British linen and silk industries were developed through an "artificial" process of import substitution, even though Britain had no comparative advantage whatsoever in these fields. As to the cotton industry that finally catapulted Britain into the industrial revolution, it began and prospered wholly behind the walls of prohibitions and high tariffs in obvious defiance of the principle of comparative advantage.

It is, therefore, reasonable to conclude that the British industrial revolution was actually begotten by trade protectionism, although it has often been argued otherwise by classical and neoclassical liberal theorists.

Although conventionally idealized as the "first industrial nation" to have modernized in an organic way, Britain, in fact, rose from underdeveloped conditions and modernized by inorganic means. Its emergence involved three revolutions. They are:

1. The revolution in economics that provided for mercantilism, a sophisticated policy tool of trade protection, wealth accumulation, industrial promotion, employment creation, state intervention, and overseas expansion all combined;

2. The revolution in proto-industrialization driven by a massive inflow of skilled labor, advanced technology, and equipment from the Continent, reflecting the dynamic interactions within the European multistate system; and

3. The revolution in finance, accelerated by the Dutch contribution, which remarkably enhanced the British state capabilities.

The British policy shift to free trade in the first half of the Nineteenth Century was by no means the result of intellectual enlightenment. As a natural outcome of the industrial supremacy that Britain now enjoyed, the free trade policy was aimed at establishing an international hierarchical order centering on Britain and serving British interests. However, the era of free trade in Europe was short-lived, since a great depression followed on the heels of the free trade movement. One country after another soon resorted to protectionism, which indeed saved them from economic difficulties and narrowed their gap with Britain.

In the meantime, free trade expanded to other parts of the world. But, insofar as it was a sort of compulsory liberalism accompanied by gun-boats, free trade in this context meant little more than colonialist and imperialist exploitation of the weak.

As an offspring of Britain born in the heyday of mercantilism, the United States of America embarked upon a road of protectionism unparalleled in terms of high tariff levels and long-term consistency. Alexan-

der Hamilton should be given adequate credit for formulating the "American System," characterized by trade protection and state intervention for industrialization. Before the Civil War, and especially after it, American industries (ranging from textiles to petroleum) underwent periods of effective protection, which enabled the country to overtake leading European powers. Only after the United States had gained overwhelming competitive advantage in most key industries did it begin to embrace the free trade doctrine in the first half of the Twentieth Century. The American experience demonstrates once again that protectionism and free trade are but two means, used in succession, to serve the end of enhancing industrial competitiveness.

The United States, since the end of the Second World War, has led the world in taking a road of trade liberalization (freer trade vs. free trade). However, even at the pinnacle of its strength, the United States did not abstain from exploiting restrictive trade legislation and policies designed to promote its security, and its political and economic interests. The relative decline of its industrial dominance in the face of the newly industrializing countries reinforced the American protectionist instinct, resulting in a proliferation of non-tariff trade barriers or even "aggressive unilateralism" under the banner of so-called "fair trade." Given these and various other double-standard trade practices by the United States, the high-sounding promise of the free trade doctrine remains as elusive as ever.

The glaring discrepancy between the free trade doctrine and the actual Anglo-Saxon practice can be accounted for by flaws in the doctrine itself. Numerous assumptions employed by free trade theorists constitute the grave weakness of the theory, rendering it largely inapplicable to the real world. A historical survey shows that valid cases against free trade have been made on grounds of terms of trade, infant industry, increasing returns, domestic distortion, and imperfect competition.

All of these challenges, in exposing loopholes of the free trade doctrine, point to the same conclusion suggested by the Anglo-Saxon experience—namely, that for any country with potential, the royal road to plenty and power is not free trading based on the principle of comparative advantage, but rather constant industrial upgrading to sustain a country's international competitive advantage.

A Christmas and New Year's Message to the Leadership and People of South Africa

Dec. 19—This message was released today in Evaton, South Africa, by Ramasimong Phillip Tsokolibane of LaRouche South Africa.

Those Who Would Divide Our Unity Would Kill Us All

Greetings and best wishes to the people of our country on behalf of Lyndon LaRouche, the American statesman and economist, who has worked tirelessly throughout his long life for the peace and progress of mankind, for the benefit of all, including all Africans, against the evil international oligarchy, headed by Her Satanic Majesty, the bitch Queen of the British Empire, and those who do her bidding, and who would gladly kill us all.

We have now reached the moment of truth in that struggle: Either we break free of the mental and economic shackles that bind us to the imperialists, or we face the likely extinction of the human species as a result of the policies of these evil beastmen. As Mr. LaRouche warned December 16,[1] the trans-Atlantic financial system—the empire of money of the City of London and Wall Street—has entered into a new and dangerous accelerating collapse process. If the world is to avoid the destructive effects of this collapse, it will require a

Citizens Electoral Council

The author addresses a conference on the BRICS, convened by the Citizens Electoral Council in Melbourne, Australia, March 29, 2015.

concerted and cooperative effort on the part of nations, including our own, to create a new, just global system, wiping out the empire of money of the imperialists, and once and for all crushing the British Empire and its agents and assets, including the mass-murdering American President Barack Obama, whom the American people must remove from office.

With that in mind, I urgently appeal to all good men and women to come together around what makes us human, to defeat the beastmen of imperialism now.

It is especially appropriate in this season, that we reflect on the fact that we, as human beings, were endowed by our Creator with the power of creativity, fundamentally and forever distinguishing us from all other living creatures. Unlike animals, we are not beasts who are victims of circumstance, but each of us, through our God-given creative powers, can discover the principles governing this universe, and by comprehending them, can deploy them to create a future for the benefit of all. In that way, each of us can make such contributions to human progress which live beyond our mortal life of flesh.

Nor, as our great accomplishments in space show us, are we bound to our cradle, this planet Earth. Our future destiny and greatness lies among the stars, beyond our Solar System, beyond even our Milky Way galaxy. We must not live by any fixed set of rules or

---

1 https://larouchepac.com/20151216/financial-crash-accelerating-fdr-would-shut-wall-street-down-fast

systems, but rather, we must constantly seek to turn the page on our as-yet-unwritten destiny. We live in the future that we create for those who come after us, believing in our own perfectibility, our ability always to advance.

This is what it means to be truly human. Those who tell us otherwise are liars, in the service of the Satanic evil that is oligarchism. Listen to your would-be leaders here in South Africa, and see if they believe that men and women are mere beasts, trapped and therefore governed, by their senses alone; and that humans are, at best, but a higher species of animals, as the environmentalists say. That is Satan using their voice! Because they deny that which makes us human, they define themselves as evil, as the enemy of mankind.

It is our human-ness that unifies us. So, therefore, anyone, any power, any "principle" that would divide the human race into "categories," "races," or "classes" as professed interest groups apart from the interest of the human race as a whole, is doing Satan's work, alienating mankind from our true identity and purpose.

Similarly, governments are constituted among men to serve the interest of the human race as a whole, deriving their mandate to exist to the extent that they succeed in establishing conditions that nurture the increasing creativity and productivity of each of its citizens. And, while governments rightly serve interests as defined within their sovereign domains, they must also serve a higher-order principle: to promote and act for the benefit of all of mankind.

We have come to the time, my friends, when conflict among sovereign interests (geopolitics) must give way to the higher interest of mankind as whole, for peace and progress to flourish. I am not speaking of some far-off, never-reached utopia, but about the here and now, when factions of imperialists, including the British puppet, U.S. President Barack Obama, are leading a drive for thermonuclear war.

As you hear or read this, we sit on the edge of the

Prince Philip, Queen Elizabeth, and their party pose with the tiger Philip had just shot, in India in 1961. He founded the World Wildlife Fund "to protect the animals" the same year. Philip cares more for animals than he does for people, yet he kills the animals.

total financial collapse of the imperialists' empire of money, the trans-Atlantic financial system. The response of the beastmen to the collapse is to seek chaos and war, with an intent to kill off as many people as possible, as rapidly as possible, which their decadent system can no longer support. *Their genocide is intentional.*

It is from the standpoint of what the human race requires now and into the future for survival—progress—that we must choose and judge our leaders, and their policies or lack of policy.

1. For example: The final document of the recently concluded COP21 UN climate change conference in Paris manifests a clear intent to impose genocide on the world. *The claim that there is any connection between actually beneficial, increasing levels of carbon dioxide and global warming is a scientific fraud,* intended to cover for genocide.

The truth is that all human progress has been defined by increases in energy-flux densities, enabling increases in energy consumption which have in turn helped to make us more productive and creative, as we have progressed from less dense fuel sources to more dense, from wood burning to coal, to fossil fuels, and now to nuclear. This is coherent with man's increasing grasp of universal principles that define this progress. Those behind the climate change hoax want to reverse our progress, demanding cuts in consumption and use of less dense energy sources such as solar and wind. If we allow this, we create a society incapable of supporting current levels of population.

The genocidal population reduction that will ensue from such evil, is consistent with the ravings of His Royal Virus, Prince Philip, the "former" Nazi, who says that people are a plague to be eliminated. He has even expressed the hope that, if reincarnated, "I would like to return as a deadly virus" so that he could kill as many people as possible!

Those who support this policy are either evil themselves or doing the work of evil.

Don't be fooled by people who say that what was agreed to in Paris, were only "voluntary" restraints that cannot be enforced. Right now, Charles, the dumbo-eared son of the bitch Queen, is working on legislation—including for South Africa and other members of the Queen's Commonwealth—that will give such agents as Prince Philip's World Wide Fund for Nature the ability to sue companies and governments to enforce compliance.

2. Or take the opposition to the proposed South African and other African nuclear programmes. Those who oppose nuclear power are also doing the work of Prince Philip. They argue that such plans are too costly.

The fact is that South Africa, to ensure an adequate supply of stable power, cannot afford not to have nuclear power. The only real problem with the government's programme, is that it accepts the environmentalist red tape that delays completion of the plants, thus artificially and unnecessarily driving up their cost. Instead, such programmes, for this country and for all Africa, should be sped up. Not only will they be a source of stable, cheap power, but they will also require the development of a skilled, African labour force for their construction and operation.

Should there be no nuclear power development in Africa, then there will be no real development, and if there is no development, Africans will die in increasing numbers. Those who oppose nuclear power are doing the deadly bidding of Satan.

3. Our government has boldly placed South Africa at the center of a global movement for a new, just world economic system, a movement based not on money and profits for an oligarchical caste, but rather on the increasing well-being and creative potential for all humankind. We are part of that 40 percent of the world's people in the BRICS alliance, consisting of Brazil, Russia, India, China, and South Africa. Its New Development Bank, with its African headquarters in Johannesburg, will distribute credit for much-needed development projects.

The BRICS initiatives are the seed crystal for a new global system to replace the dying empire of money. Much more needs to be done to bring all of this to realisation, but no sane person can oppose South Africa's participation in the BRICS. Those who do so, for whatever reason, are not only wrong; they are doing service for the imperialists and their proposed genocide, by dividing us from our allies in human progress.

4. It has been the policy of the British Empire to oppose any initiative that might destroy its ability to rule. Using its American assets, which include President Obama, and its Wall Street satrapy, it funds subversive and destructive activities against targeted nations, governments, and individuals. It promotes terrorism and chaos, and otherwise undermines legitimate governments' ability to govern. It side-tracks initiatives that threaten imperial policy. It seeks to divide governments and their peoples to rage against each other.

We must look carefully at the recent unrest in our country and the calls for regime change. At root, these come from the imperialists. To those who say that they wish to force a change in government, please ask them what their policies are on the critical issues of the day that we speak of here. Their silence on exposing the global warming hoax, their silence on nuclear energy, and on the BRICS, should forewarn us that evil is afoot here.

Think not of partisan politics or even the national interest in making your judgments. Think of the common aims of mankind. We must rise to the as-yet-unfulfilled promise of the opportunity given us by Nelson Mandela, who called on us to be a great people, taking into our hearts the aspirations not only of those now living, but also of future generations. Let us ask ourselves how our posterity will judge us—if we, by our actions today, have given them that future opportunity.

God bless all of you! Peace!

www.ingramcontent.com/pod-product-compliance
Lightning Source LLC
Chambersburg PA
CBHW080834310526
45788CB00020B/3527